FIRST GRADE

TIMBERDOODLE'S
CURRICULUM HANDBOOK

2020-2021 EDITION

"WHALE" COVER ART BY SHERI AND JOE K.
"EGYPTIAN PHARAOH" COVER ART BY SHERI K.
ALL THE AMAZING INTERIOR DOODLES PROVIDED BY OUR TALENTED CUSTOMERS

Welcome to First Grade

WE'RE SO GLAD YOU'RE HERE!

Congratulations on choosing to homeschool this year! Whether this is your first year as a teacher or your tenth, we're confident you'll find that there is very little that compares to watching your child's learning take off. In fact, teaching can be quite addictive, so be forewarned!

ON YOUR MARK, GET SET, GO!

Preparing for your first "school day" is very easy. Peruse this guide, look over the typical schedule, browse the introductions in your books, and you will be ready to go.

GET SUPPORT

Are you looking for a place to hang out online with like-minded homeschoolers? Do you wonder how someone else handled a particular science experiment? Or do you wish you could encourage someone who is just getting started this year? Join one or more of our Facebook groups.

Timberdoodlers of all ages:
https://www.facebook.com/groups/Timberdoodle/

Timberdoodlers with 1st- to 4th-grade students:
www.facebook.com/groups/ElementaryTimberdoodle

SCHEDULE CUSTOMIZER

Your 2020–2021 First-Grade Curriculum Kit includes access to our Schedule Customizer where you can not only adjust the school weeks but also tweak the checklist to include exactly what you want on your schedule. To get started, just click the link in your access email and visit the scheduling website!
www.TimberdoodleSchedules.com

If you ordered through a charter school or don't have that link for some other reason, just email schedules@Timberdoodle.com and we'll get that sorted out ASAP. (Including your order number will really speed that process up for you.)

WE WILL HELP

We would love to assist you if questions come up, so please don't hesitate to contact us with any questions, comments, or concerns. Whether you contact us by phone, email, or live online chat, you will get a real person who is eager to serve you and your family.

YOU WILL LOVE THIS!

This year you and your student will learn more than you hoped while having a blast. Ready? Have an absolutely amazing year!

CONTENTS

MEET YOUR HANDBOOK

WELCOME TO YOUR TEACHING TOOLBOX!

Simple Is Better
We really believe that, so your guide is as simple as we could make it.

1. The Planning
First up are all the details on planning your year, including your annual planner and sample weekly checklists, the absolute backbones of Timberdoodle's curriculum kits. More on those in a moment.

2. Reading Challenge
Next up is the reading challenge, complete with book ideas to give you a head start.

3. Item-by-Item Details
We then include short bios of each item in your kit, ideal for refreshing your memory on why each is included or to show off exactly what your first-grader will be covering this year. This is where we've tucked in our tips or tricks to make this year more awesome for all of you.

4. Teacher Resources
In this section you'll find our favorite articles and tidbits amassed in our more-than-30 years of homeschool experience.

5. Items with Special Instructions
Here you'll find 52 ideas for using Mad Mattr, suggestions for Imagidice Story Cubes, and models to build using Plus-Plus.

6. Book Suggestions
Finally, we'll conclude with specific book ideas for your reading challenge this year.

All the Details Included
This Timberdoodle curriculum kit is available in three different standard levels: Basic, Complete, or Elite. This allows you to choose the assortment best suited to your child's interest level, your family's schedule, and your budget. In this guide, you'll find an overview and any tips for each of the items included in the Elite Curriculum Kit. If you purchased a Basic or Complete kit, or if you customized your kit, you chose not to receive every item, so you'll only need to familiarize yourself with the ones which were included in your kit.

Don't Panic, You Didn't Order Too Much Stuff!
We know you. OK, maybe not you personally, but we have yet to meet a homeschooler who doesn't have other irons in the fire. From homesteading or running a business to swimming lessons or doctor's appointments, your weeks are not dull. As you unpack your box you may be asking yourself how you'll ever fit it all in.

We'll go in-depth on schedules momentarily, but for now know that most of the items in your kit feature short lessons, not all of them should be done every day, and your checklist is going to make this incredibly manageable. Really!

TIPS & TRICKS

YOUR FIRST WEEK, STATE LAWS, AND MORE

Week 1 Hints

As you get started this year, realize that you are just getting your sea legs. Expect your studies to take a little longer and be a little less smooth than they will be by the end of the year. As you get your feet under you, you will discover the rhythm that works best for you! If you don't know where to begin each day, why not try starting with something from the Thinking Skills category? It will get your child's brain in gear and set a great tone for the rest of the day.

Find Your Pace

We asked parents who used this kit how long their students spent on "school." About 74% said that they spent 2–4 hours a day using their Timberdoodle First-Grade Kit. That is not only a wide variation, but it also means some were outside that window. Make sure you allow yourself and your child some time to find your own rhythm!

Books First, or Not?

Some goal-oriented students might like to start each day with bookwork

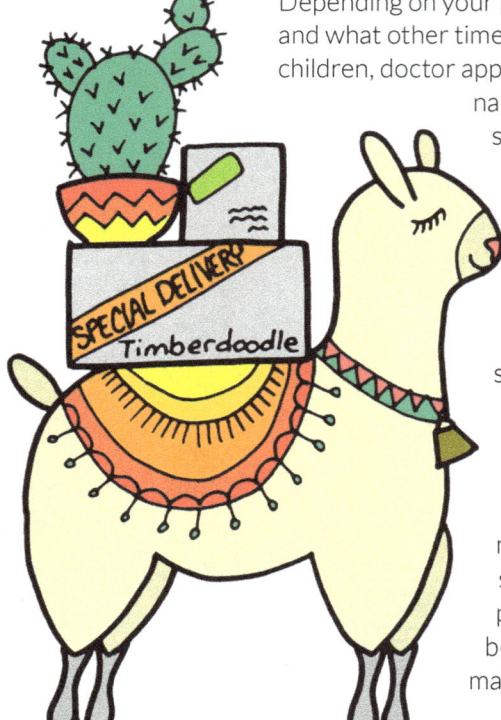

and end with fun, hands-on time. Others might prefer to intersperse the hands-on thinking games, STEM, and so forth between more intensive subjects to give their brains a clean slate.

A Little Every Day, or All at Once?

Depending on your preferences, your child's attention span, and what other time commitments you have (teaching other children, doctor appointments, working around a baby's nap), there are many different ways to schedule your week. Some families like to do a little portion from nearly all subjects every day, while others prefer to blast out an entire week's work within a subject in a single sitting. Throughout the year, you can tinker around with your daily scheduling and see what approach works best for your family.

Tips for Newbies

If you're new to homeschooling, it might be helpful for you to know that some subjects are typically taught and practiced several times a week for the best mastery. These would include basic math instruction, phonics, and spelling.

However, more topical subjects such as geography, history, and science are often taught all at once. Meanwhile, thinking skills, STEM, and art, plus hands-on learning and games, can be even more tailored to the preferences of the child or used for independent learning while you are busy.

What About the Courses Which You Don't Work on Every Week?

As you go over your checklist, you'll notice that some of your courses are "2–3 a month" or "as desired," and that may leave you confused on how to tackle them. Here are a few other options: You could go ahead and do it every week, completing the course early. You could set aside the item for summer (see below). Or you could complete it as directed, of course!

The Summer Plan

If you're looking at all these tools and feeling a little overwhelmed, or if you just wish you had more structured activities for the summer, feel free to grab a handful of items from the kit and set them aside for summer. Then, set a reminder on your phone or calendar to remind you which ones they are and where you stashed them so you won't forget to use them!

Continued on the next page.

TIPS & TRICKS, CONT.

Meeting State Requirements

Check https://www.hslda.org/laws to see the most current information on your specific requirements. For many states, it is sufficient to simply hang on to your completed and dated weekly checklists along with a sampling of your child's best work this year. Some states ask you to add in a state-specific topic or two, such as Vermont history, or a generic course like P.E. or health. We have a summary on our blog comparing your kit to their requirements, but HSLDA is the gold standard for current legal information.

P.E.? Health?

We suggest thinking outside the box on this. Many of the science courses have a health component that meets the requirement. P.E. is a great way to fit your child's favorite activity into the school schedule. Ballet, soccer, horseback riding, swimming... there are so many fun ways to check off P.E. this year!

Put Your Child in Charge?

The weekly checklists are the framework of your week, designed for maximum flexibility. Just check off each item as you get it done for the week and you'll be able to see at a glance that you still need to do _____ this week. (This is true of the daily checklists as well–just on a shorter schedule.) Many students even prefer to get all their work done early in the week and enjoy all their leisure time at once!

Do Hard Things and Easy Ones

Our family provides foster care for kids who need a safe place for a while. This has exposed us to a whole new world of hard days and stressful weeks. If your child is struggling today, you are not failing if you take a step back and have him start with his most calming project. For our crew, often that would be art or the reading challenge. You even have a little slush room in most subjects, so don't hesitate to trim

the lessons short on a busy or challenging week, or pause schoolwork today for a complete reset and tackle it fresh tomorrow.

At the same time, you are not doing your child any favors if you never teach him how to work through a challenge. After all, you have hard days as a parent and still get up, drink your coffee, and jump back in. Be aware of your own tendency to have your child either buckle down and push through or to let him ease off completely, then work to provide a healthy balance for your child, particularly if he is in the process of healing.

Pro Tip

When you first get out a week's checklist, go ahead and check off all the things you don't need to do this week. For instance, if your child did a few extra pages of math last week or you are putting off all art kits until winter, check those off. Doesn't that feel better?

The Sample Schedules

We're including a sample annual planner on page 18, followed by sample weekly planners for each level of your kit, reflecting a typical 36-week school year. This lets you see at a glance how this might work for you, even before you get a moment to sit down at your computer and print your own custom-fitted schedule.

ASK YOUR FIRST-GRADER!

A JUST-FOR-FUN BEGINNING OF THE YEAR INTERVIEW

Jot down your child's answers here to capture a fun time capsule of his first-grade year.

1. What's your favorite food? (How do you make it?)

2. What do you want to be when you grow up?

3. What would you put into a treasure box?

4. What are your (homeschool) teacher's favorite things to do?

5. What does your (homeschool) teacher say the most?

6. If you were to go on an adventure, where would you go or what would you do?

7. If we found the perfect book at the library for you, what would it be about?

8. What kind of vacation would you like to go on? Or what is the favorite one you have been on?

9. What is your favorite animal?

10. What is your favorite thing to do?

11. What's the best thing you've ever learned?

12. What is going to be the best part of first grade?

A SELF-PORTRAIT (OR PHOTO) OF _____

MEET YOUR ONLINE SCHEDULER

GETTING THE MOST OUT OF YOUR PLANNERS

Use the Customizer

On the next pages you'll find sample weekly checklists for Basic, Complete, and Elite kits. Before you photocopy 36 of them, though, take a moment to check out the custom online schedule builder that came free with your kit. You'll not only easily adjust the weeks, but you'll also tweak the checklist to include exactly what you want listed. Plus, you'll be able to print your weekly checklists directly from the schedule builder so you don't have to do that by photocopying! www.TimberdoodleSchedules.com

Activating Your Account

Before you can get started, you'll need your account activated for the online schedule builder. If you didn't get an activation email (perhaps you ordered through a charter school so we didn't have your email address), shoot us a quick email at schedules@Timberdoodle.com and we'll get that straightened out ASAP. Including your order number really speeds that process up, but our team is skilled at finding your activation info with whatever order data you have.

What's Your Dream Schedule?

Now that you're ready you'll want to know two things:

1. How Many Weeks Do You Want to Do School?

A standard school year is 36 weeks + breaks. Some families prefer to expedite and complete the entire year in fewer weeks—a great option for those of you who'd like to get all this year's school done before baby arrives, for instance. Or perhaps your family, like ours, prefers to school year-round and keep that brain sharp.

2. What Breaks Do You Want?

Thanksgiving, Christmas, winter break, spring break... you could also add in weeks off that you're traveling, have guests, baby is coming, or...

Typically you'll be adding full-week breaks only, so unless you're traveling to Disneyland® for little Johnny's birthday, you don't need to add that to the calendar. For single-day breaks you'll likely prefer to just shuffle the work to earlier/later in the same week and keep on task otherwise. If you're using a daily schedule (next page), though, you may find it worth your time to enter days off, as well.

Choosing Your Items

Now just pop that data into the online schedule and scroll down to see the items you might have in your kit. Unchecking the boxes for any items you don't have removes them from your list. You'll also see "Alternative Items" listed under each subject. This usually includes all of our most popular customizations for this grade so that you can simply check a box and switch the scheduler to an upper or lower case math, for instance.

Add Custom Courses

Your course list is limited only by your imagination. Perhaps your friend wrote you a custom curriculum you'd like to include, your family makes up a band and you'd like to have practice on this list, or you need to list ballet since that's P.E.

this year. At the very bottom of the page you'll find a place to add in just as many courses as you'd like. Just walk through the prompts on-screen to get it all set up.

Tweak It to Perfection

Do you have everything set? On the next screen you'll have some fun options.

Continued on the next page.

MEET YOUR ONLINE SCHEDULER, CONT.

1. Large-Font Edition
Want a large-font option? Just check the box. If you don't like how it looks you can always come back and uncheck it.

2. Show Dates
Check this box if it's helpful for you to see at a glance that week 17 is January 13th–17th, for instance. Some teachers find this incredibly helpful while others prefer to move breaks around on the fly, making the dates irrelevant.

3. Weekly or Daily?
We prefer a weekly schedule, for the simple reason that our weeks are rarely without some anomaly. Off to the dentist's Tuesday? You won't fall behind by taking a day off.

Or perhaps you have Friday Robotics Camp for a couple of weeks and need to get all the week's work done over four days instead of five. No problem! This approach also teaches time-management skills (see the article on Independent Learning at the back of this book).

However, we've heard from many of you that having a daily schedule, especially for the first month, is a real life-saver. So we developed one for you, and if it helps you, fantastic! The daily scheduler is programmed to split up the work as evenly as possible over the week, with the beginning of the week having any extra pages or lessons. (We all know that end-of-the-week doldrums are a real thing!)

Moving Courses to Certain Days
If you're opting for the daily scheduler, you do have some helpful fine-tuning options. Just click "Edit" on the course in question and you'll have the option of selecting on which days of the week the course will appear. This lets you do things like schedule history only on Wednesday because that is co-op day. Or, you could schedule science only on Tuesday or Thursday and STEM on Friday or Monday so that science and STEM are never on the same day.

Pro Tip
You can also opt to exclude an item from certain weeks. This is useful if you already know that you want to save an art kit for May so that Grandma can do it with Johnny or if you don't want to break out the graphic novel until after Christmas since you've set it aside as a gift.

4. Show Unit Range?
This feature sounds so very data-y and not super helpful, but we think you just might love it. Instead of saying that you

need to do seven pages of math this week, check this box to have it remind you that you're on worksheets 50–56 this week, for example. If you prefer extreme flexibility, leave this box unchecked. But if you're afraid of falling behind without knowing it, this box will be your hero.

Make More Lists
If you have one student and one teacher, you may feel free to buzz past this idea. But if you have an extra teacher–perhaps your spouse, a grandparent, or even an older sibling who wants the bonding time, then this may simplify your life! Instead of putting all of your child's work on a single list, you could put all the subjects you will teach on your list and all of the remaining subjects on "Grandma's list" for her ease.

If you have twins or multiple students at the same grade level, you can also make multiple lists to best meet each student's needs.

That's It!
Click Generate Schedule, then View Generated Schedule and you're ready to print it and get started!

FYI, our scheduler is constantly being improved, so for the most current instructions please refer to the blog link in your activation email.

Ideas Our Team Is Working On
At the time of this printing, our team is working to add a time log to these lists for those of you whose states require it. We're also adding a way to easily email the schedule to yourself for your record, adding a progress report, and

fine-tuning how you add time off to your schedule. These are all features that you may expect to see more about on the above-mentioned blog. Also, please let us know if you think of more features that our team should consider!

	CURRICULUM	LESSONS OR PAGES	= PER WEEK
Language Arts	All About Reading Level 2	54 lessons	20 minutes a day
	Daily 6-Trait Writing	25 weeks	1 week's work
	Spelling You See B	36 weeks	1 week's work
	Imagidice	unlimited	once a week
Math	Math-U-See	30 lessons	a 7-worksheet lesson
	Wrap-ups Addition & Subtraction	20 boards	once a week
	Möbi Kids	unlimited	once a week
Thinking Skills	Critical & Creative 1	71 double-sided pages	2 double-sided pages
	miniLUK Set A or Sets A & B	98 or 280 challenges	3 or 8 challenges
	Smart Cookies	64 challenges	2 challenges
	Postman Observation Game	unlimited	once a week
History & Social Studies	The Story of the World 1	42 chapters	1–2 chapters
	Skill Sharpeners Geography	135 pages	4 pages
	ScrunchMap World	unlimited	unlimited
	Famous Figures of Ancient Times	20 figures	2–3 per month
Science	Science in the Beginning	90 lessons	2–3 lessons
STEM	Plus-Plus 1,200 with baseplate	unlimited	2+ models
	Robotis Pets	7 models	as desired
Art	What's New? What's Missing? What's Different?	42 spreads	1–2 spreads
	Aquarellum Cosmos	2 paintings	as desired
	Doodle Washington D.C.	95 doodles	2–3 doodles
	Cosmos Foil	12 projects	as desired
	Do Art Coloring with Clay	4 projects	as desired
Etc.	Mad Mattr Craftsman	unlimited	as desired
	Test Prep	128 pages	end of school year

WHAT IS A LESSON?

ITEM BY ITEM SPECS

On pages 34–69 you'll find an overview of each item, including information about how we split up the work and why, but if you're looking for a quick reference guide to refresh your mind on what exactly "one lesson" means for any of your materials, here you go!

All About Reading Level 2
Time based—just do 20 minutes a day.

Daily 6-Trait Writing
The course is split into 25 weeks of work. We suggest starting this after 11 weeks of school to make sure your student is ready.

Spelling You See B
There are 36 lessons, each of which includes five days of work. Two tips: Your day's lesson is complete after 10 minutes of work—your child does not need to finish that whole chunk. Also, if you're using a four-day week or otherwise don't get to all five days of work in a week, it is expected the you will still count that lesson as complete at the end of the week and move to the next one.

Imagidice
Unlimited. We suggest pulling it out at least once a week. Check out all the ideas on how to use it on pages 92–93.

Math-U-See
You'll find 30 lessons here, each with seven worksheets. Since you'll only be completing as many of the worksheets as your child needs per lesson, and since completing one whole lesson a week keeps the instructional portions predictable, we suggest doing one lesson a week instead of a certain number of worksheets. If you use that method, know that you can spread a tricky lesson over two weeks up to six times this year without messing up your schedule.

We do still provide you with seven checkboxes a week so that your child doesn't have to fully complete his lesson to log the significant progress he's made. Just plan to check off any worksheets you're skipping this week and it will work perfectly.

Wrap-ups Addition & Subtraction
Unlimited. We suggest twice a week until your child masters the drill work.

Möbi Kids Game
Unlimited. We suggest pulling it out at least once a week.

Critical & Creative 1
The easiest way to use this book is simply to rip out two double-sided pages a week for your child to complete.

miniLUK Sets A & B
If you have Set A, add three new challenges/pages a week. If you have both sets, though, you may add eight challenges a week!

Smart Cookies
Just do two new challenges a week, adding in as many "old" ones as your child would like.

Postman Observation Game
Unlimited. Like the other games, we suggest pulling it out at least once a week.

The Story of the World 1

With 42 chapters, you're going to want to do three chapters every two weeks. Or, if it's easier, just do two chapters one week and 1 chapter the following week. Add in as many activities as you have the time/interest for.

Skill Sharpeners Geography

Simply complete about 4 pages a week.

ScrunchMap World

Unlimited - we suggest pulling it out at least once a week.

Famous Figures of Ancient Times

There are 10 models to complete, each with a full-color and a color-it-yourself option. See page 54 for where those figures appear in Story of the World or just add one to your studies each month.

Science in the Beginning

You'll see that some of the lessons in this book are color-coded red. These are optional lessons, so if you're trying to streamline your days, feel free to skip those and only do two lessons a week. If you want to do all the lessons, plan on three a week. If you purchased the Elite kit, use your lab set for easy experiments.

Plus-Plus 1,200 with baseplate

Unlimited. We recommend completing the 36-week Plus-Plus challenge which begins on page 100. This gives your child two new models a week. If he finds some models tricky, make sure he reviews the "how to build" instructions on page 127 and following.

Robotis Pets

There are seven models to complete, so we suggest one a month. This could be completed in installments or all at once, depending on what works best for your child.

What's New? What's Missing? What's Different?

This book has 42 spreads, each with varying amounts of work. We'd suggest completing 1–2 spreads a week, but consider breaking that up over multiple days. Some of the pages have a lot of different drawing or thinking activities. This could be overwhelming for a first-grader to do in one sitting but much more fun to do a little each day.

Aquarellum Cosmos

There are only two paintings to complete, but these have the potential to be intricate masterpieces. If you and your child have the patience to pull it out over and over, do it. Just 15 focused minutes a week will give you some amazing results.

Doodle Washington D.C.

There are 95 doodles to complete in this book. Many span two pages, but others stand-alone. Just complete two to three doodles a week regardless of how many spreads that is, and you'll finish them all this year.

Cosmos Foil

Use as desired or complete one every three weeks.

Do Art Coloring with Clay

This kit has four art projects, and each would do well as a rainy-day project or a work of art done in stages if you prefer.

Mad Mattr Craftsman

Use when desired as a fidget, or assign it once a week as a sensory tool. You decide!

Test Prep

We usually save this for the end of the year to refresh the student on all the skills he'll need for annual testing. You won't find this on your schedule unless you add it.

Language Arts	All About Reading Level 2	20 minutes a day								
	Daily 6-Trait Writing	1 week's work								
	Spelling You See B	1 week's work								
Math	Math-U-See	a 7-worksheet lesson								
Thinking Skills	Critical & Creative 1	2 double-sided pages								
Art	What's New? What's Missing? What's Different?	1–2 spreads								

Category	Item	Frequency					
Language Arts	All About Reading Level 2	20 minutes a day					
Language Arts	Daily 6-Trait Writing	1 week's work					
Language Arts	Spelling You See B	1 week's work					
Language Arts	Imagidice	once a week					
Math	Math-U-See	a 7-worksheet lesson					
Math	Wrap-ups Addition & Subtraction	once a week					
Thinking Skills	Critical & Creative 1	2 double-sided pages					
Thinking Skills	miniLUK Set A	3 challenges					
Thinking Skills	Smart Cookies	2 challenges					
History & Social Studies	The Story of the World 1	1–2 chapters					
History & Social Studies	Skill Sharpeners Geography	4 pages					
History & Social Studies	ScrunchMap World	unlimited					
Science	Science in the Beginning	2–3 lessons					
STEM	Plus-Plus 1,200 with baseplate	2+ models					
Art	What's New? What's Missing? What's Different?	1–2 spreads					
Art	Aquarellum Cosmos	as desired					
Art	Doodle Washington D.C.	2–3 doodles					
Etc.	Mad Mattr Craftsman	at least once a week					

Language Arts	All About Reading Level 2	20 minutes a day						
	Daily 6-Trait Writing	1 week's work						
	Spelling You See B	1 week's work						
	Imagidice	once a week						
Math	Math-U-See	a 7-worksheet lesson						
	Wrap-ups Addition & Subtraction	once a week						
	Möbi Kids	once a week						
Thinking Skills	Critical & Creative 1	2 double-sided pages						
	miniLÜK Sets A & B	8 challenges						
	Smart Cookies	2 challenges						
	Postman Observation Game	once a week						
History & Social Studies	The Story of the World 1	1–2 chapters						
	Skill Sharpeners Geography	4 pages						
	ScrunchMap World	unlimited						
	Famous Figures of Ancient Times	2–3 per month						
Science	Science in the Beginning	2–3 lessons						
STEM	Plus-Plus 1,200 with baseplate	2+ models						
	Robotis Pets	as desired						
Art	What's New? What's Missing? What's Different?	1–2 spreads						
	Aquarellum Cosmos	as desired						
	Doodle Washington D.C.	2–3 doodles						
	Cosmos Foil	as desired						
	Do Art Coloring with Clay	as desired						
Etc.	Mad Mattr Craftsman	at least once a week						

WEEKLY CHECKLIST (ELITE)

THE READING CHALLENGE

BASED ON THE READING CHALLENGE FOR KIDS FROM REDEEMEDREADER.COM

The Reading Challenge for Kids will get you and your child reading a broader variety of books this year and perhaps discovering new favorites. This reading challenge is heavily adapted by us and used with permission from the fine folks at RedeemedReader.com. Check out their website for more information about this reading challenge and for great book reviews and book suggestions for your kids.

Reading Solo and Together

At this grade level a few students will read most of these books independently while most are still building their independent reading skills. Many parents will plan to be doing the bulk of the reading this year. However, even if your child is ready to take off independently, we highly recommend keeping a read-aloud time too, just as long as it's possible. Many sources recommend that parents continue reading to their children well past the time their children become accomplished readers, and we agree!

How It Works

On the following pages, you'll find four lists of books which you are meant to read one after another this year. Not all families will make it through all the lists, so you will need to choose a reading goal early in the year and set your pace accordingly.

The Light Reader plan has 13 books, which sets a pace of one book every four weeks. The majority of families can and should do at least this much.

The Avid Reader plan adds another 13 books, which increases the pace to one book every two weeks. This is doable for most families.

The Committed Reader plan adds a further 26 books, bringing the total to 52, or one book every week. By including picture books, we think that even this faster pace is not too rigorous and is suitable for enthusiastic readers with time in their schedules.

The Obsessed Reader plan doubles the total yet again, bringing it to 104 books, which sets a pace of two books every week. We highly recommend this challenge, but it may be too intense for families with already-packed schedules!

Getting Started

Begin with the Light plan, which includes suggestions for 13 books. Choose those books and read them in any order, checking them off as you complete them.

Next, advance to the Avid plan, using the criteria there to choose another 13 books and read them in any order.

Then it's time to move to the Committed plan with a further 26 books, again reading them in any order.

If you have completed the Committed plan (that's 52 books so far!), you are ready to brave the Obsessed plan.

If you want to finish your books in a school year rather than in an entire calendar year, the timeline shifts a bit, so be sure to set your goal at the beginning of the year and pace yourself accordingly.

Here's the pace for a 36-week schedule:

Light Reader: One book every two to three weeks.

Avid Reader: One book every week or two.

Committed Reader: One and a half books every week.

Obsessed Reader: Almost three books every week.

How Long Do We Count Picture Books?

I recently heard this beautiful quote from Sarah Mackenzie at the Read-Aloud Revival:

"Another thing I want to point out is picture books. As your child grows older, do not stop reading picture books. Picture books are written, often times, with more eloquent, beautiful language than chapter books or middle-grade novels so the reading level in the picture book is actually higher than it is in the novel. A beautifully written picture book is like poetry and an art gallery combined into one. So they are not less than, or they're not inferior to longer novels. The beautiful thing about picture books is because they're short, you can experience more stories this way. So if you prioritize picture books over novels when it comes to reading aloud, you will actually fill your child's memories and childhood with more stories..." (Hear the whole conversation on the Read-Aloud Revival podcast, at the beginning of episode 121.)

But I Don't Have Any Idea Which Books to Choose!

We have your back! Beginning on page 140 you'll find hundreds of book ideas you'll love this year.

If you want more ideas, we highly recommend your local librarian, the Read-Aloud Revival podcast, and the Timberdoodle Facebook groups as excellent starting points. It's also a wonderful idea to peek at the additional reading ideas in your history or science textbooks – particularly if your child was fascinated by something his courses recently touched on.

Will This Be Expensive?

It doesn't need to be. You can read library books, buy used, borrow from friends, and scour your family bookshelves. Don't forget that many libraries have free e-versions, as well. It doesn't get much more convenient than that!

But How Do I Fit This Much Reading Into My Day?

Here are nine ideas to incorporate more reading into your family's busy schedule and unique schooling style:

1. Use Books of Various Lengths

A longer book than you'd usually pick may be perfect as an audio book. On the flip side, if your child will be be reading to a younger sibling or you are picking a new readaloud for the whole gang, feel free to gear the book towards the younger participants, particularly if you're short on time. Picture books allow for more stories in less time, but they don't lack at all for impact.

2. Assign Independent Reading

This can be done in conjunction with quiet time or simply throughout the day. Our household often uses it as a strategy to calm the hyper and soothe the sad—"I need you to go read one book (or one chapter) and then come back and we'll try again." Even a child who is not yet a fluent reader will benefit from some time to study his favorite picture books.

3. Quiet Time!

Does your family implement a quiet time already? Reading is a natural perk for that time. Quiet time can be as simple as setting a timer for 30 minutes (or more) and having your child relax with his favorite blanket or weighted lap pad and, of course, his book. If it's possible for you to grab a book that you've been wanting to read and embrace the same plan, you'll be modeling what an ageless wonder reading can be. Of course, if your household is filled with little ones, it may be more practical for you to use this time for feeding babies or fixing dinner and there's no shame in that, but consider your options as you plan your year.

4. Sneak Reading Into Your Existing Routines

What routines are already going well for you? Could you incorporate a reading time right into your existing bedtime routine, family devotions, car time, snack time, or other routine?

5. Audiobooks

Incorporate audiobooks and save the designated reader some time and energy. This is a particularly spectacular move for car time, art time, puzzle time, or even to smooth over particularly grumpy mealtimes.

6. Put the Busy Ones to Work

Encourage quiet activities such as puzzles, this year's STEM kit, or coloring while you read aloud or play the audiobook. It can be legitimately impossible for your kinesthetic learner to sit perfectly still and listen angelically, but break out the "listening time only" tools and suddenly everyone looks forward to reading!

7. Brothers and Sisters

You don't have to be the only one reading with your child. Have your "big kid" read to a younger sibling as part of their school lessons. The older sibling will gain fluency as your younger one soaks up the one-on-one time. Or have your beginning reader share his favorite books with an older sibling! (No siblings in your home? How about cousins, playmates, grandparents, or even the family pet?)

8. Grandpa, Grandma, Aunties, Oh My!

Perhaps an auntie would welcome the opportunity to have Friday evenings be read-aloud time, complete with hot cocoa and scones. Or Grandma might love the idea of hosting all of her grandchildren once a month for a giant book party—each child could bring his favorite book to share. Too far away? Grandpa could record his favorite book (any audio-recording app should work), then send the book to your child so that he can read along with Grandpa.

9. Get a Library Routine Going

Our family has loved reading since our toddler days, but we didn't use the library well until we settled into a simple routine. For us that involves a central location for all library books and having a designated person willing to return current books and pick up the holds each week. Those simple steps have quickly borne fruit with many more hours spent reading "new" books!

Let's Read!

Pick your plan, choose some books with your child, and get started!

THE LIGHT READER

The Challenge	The Book You Chose	Date Completed
1. A book about being a Christian or about what the Bible teaches		
2. A book about the world		
3. A biography		
4. A classic novel/story		
5. A book your grandparent (or other relative) says was his/her favorite at your age		
6. A book from the Old Testament (or a retelling of an Old Testament story)		
7. A book from the New Testament (or a retelling of a New Testament story)		
8. A book based on a true story		
9. A book your pastor or Sunday School teacher recommends		
10. A book more than 100 years old		
11. A book about families		
12. A book about relationships or friendship		
13. A book featuring someone of a different ethnicity than you		

THE AVID READER

The Challenge	The Book You Chose	Date Completed
14. A book about someone who came from another country		
15. A book of fairy tales or folk tales (or an extended retelling of one)		
16. A book recommended by a parent or sibling		
17. A book by or about a missionary		
18. A Caldecott, Newbery, or Geisel Award winner		
19. A book about a holiday		
20. A book about grandparents		
21. A book with visual puzzles		
22. A book that has a fruit of the Spirit in its title		
23. A book about a farm		
24. A book about illness or medicine		
25. A book about school, a teacher, or learning		
26. A graphic novel		

The Challenge	The Book You Chose	Date Completed
27. A book of poetry		
28. A book with a great cover		
29. A book about food		
30. A book about weather		
31. A book about an adventure		
32. A book by or about William Shakespeare (or a retelling of one of his plays)		
33. A funny book		
34. A mystery or detective story		
35. An easy reader classic (e.g., A Bargain for Frances, Frog and Toad, Little Bear, etc.)		
36. A book by or about a famous American		
37. A book about ancient history		
38. A book about medieval history		
39. A book about money		

The Challenge	The Book You Chose	Date Completed
40. A book about art or artists		
41. A book about music or a musician		
42. A book about an invention or inventor		
43. A book about feelings or emotions		
44. A book about a boy		
45. A book about a girl		
46. A book about books, libraries, or learning to read		
47. A book about adoption		
48. A book about someone who is differently abled (blind, deaf, mentally handicapped, etc.)		
49. A book you or your family owns but you've never read		
50. A book about babies		
51. A book about writing		
52. A book made into a movie (but read the book first!)		

The Challenge	The Book You Chose	Date Completed
53. A book about prayer		
54. A book recommended by a librarian or teacher		
55. An encyclopedia, dictionary, or almanac		
56. A book about construction		
57. A biography of a world leader		
58. A book published the same year you (the student) were born		
59. A book with a one-word title		
60. A book about service		
61. A book about siblings		
62. A book about animals		
63. A book featuring a dog		
64. A book featuring a cat		
65. A wordless book		
66. A book about plants or gardening		
67. A book about a hobby or a skill you want to learn		
68. A book of comics		
69. A book about a famous war		
70. A book about sports		
71. A book about math (numbers, mathematicians, patterns...)		
72. A book about suffering or poverty		
73. A book by your favorite author		
74. A book you've read before		
75. A book with an ugly cover		
76. A book about someone else's favorite subject		
77. A book about travel or transportation		
78. A book about the natural world		

The Challenge	The Book You Chose	Date Completed
79. A biography of an author		
80. A book published in 2020-2021		
81. A historical fiction book		
82. A book about science or a scientist		
83. A book about safety or survival		
84. A book about space or an astronaut		
85. A book set in Central or South America		
86. A book set in Africa		
87. A book set in Asia		
88. A book set in Europe		
89. A book with a color in its title		
90. A book about manners		
91. A book about spring		
92. A book about summer		
93. A book about autumn		
94. A book about winter		
95. A book about home		
96. A book about bears		
97. A book about your body		
98. A book starring community helpers		
99. A book featuring a bird or birds		
100. A book about a zoo		
101. A book about the ocean		
102. A book with jungle animals		
103. A book about something that makes you happy		
104. A book about your state or region		

BEGINNING READING, WRITING, SPELLING, AND STORIES

This year your child will progress a long way in his reading abilities. Watch for three-letter blends, the jobs of Silent E, new phonograms, and methods for decoding multisyllable words.

Spelling is included primarily because Spelling You See is a magnificent way to reinforce the phonics you're studying in All About Reading, in just 10 minutes a day.

With 6-Trait Writing your child will begin to develop into a skilled writer using short and engaging lessons.

Finally, Imagidice adds a game aspect to teaching good story telling. Look for additional ways to play at the back of this handbook.

YOU GET TO TEACH READING!

THIS MAY BE THE BEST PART OF TEACHING FIRST GRADE

Seeing a child go from having no reading abilities (or limited reading abilities) to being a fully competent, even eager reader has been the highlight of many a teaching parent! In fact, helping him become a competent and comfortable reader is one of your biggest goals this year. So how do you facilitate that?

1) Make It Immediately Rewarding

Whether he is a natural reader or one who will take a few years to fully master this skill, it is critical to make reading as fun and rewarding as possible now. Reading is naturally exciting, so all you are going to need to do is allow him to experience this thrill himself! Beyond food rewards (we're not above using them, if they really help!), one of the simplest, most universally appealing techniques is to get him reading "real books" just as soon as possible. Use the readers included, but also supplement with library books that suit his interests and current skill.

2) Read Together

Just because he's beginning to read doesn't mean that his literature intake should be limited to short phonetic books. Foster his love of literature by frequently reading books aloud that interest him and discussing them together, just as you've been doing. (See the Reading Challenge on page 24, as well.)

3) Write Slowly

Take a good look at your child's abilities and writing readiness before insisting that he complete any of these written lessons. Some children develop their fine motor skills more slowly than others, and those children benefit most from simply setting the workbooks aside and taking some time to develop before tackling them again. Making it a discipline issue when it's really a developmental issue benefits no one.

If your child is ready for the content of the books but the writing is holding him back or making them tedious for him, here are a couple of options to try:

- Have him write the answer on a chalkboard or other larger surface.

- Spread shaving cream over the table and let him write answers in it using his finger or a paintbrush.

- Fill a shallow tray with salt and let him write answers there. You can copy them to his paper for him.

Any of these options turn the challenging fine motor task into a slightly easier yet still skill-building opportunity. Or, of course, you could sign yourself up as scribe for the day and write down the answers he dictates for you!

ALL ABOUT READING

BASIC ~ COMPLETE ~ ELITE

The backbone of this year's language arts is All About Reading, the multisensory, mastery-based program that you've been hearing so much about. Suitable for all learning styles, AAR teaches phonics, decoding, fluency, and comprehension in a fun and engaging way.

Moving at a gentler pace than other more intense reading programs, with AAR only one new concept is taught at a time. Their precept-upon-precept program works with almost all students, and AAR's built-in review system helps learning to stick.

You will be thrilled to know that no prior training is needed;

AAR has lightly scripted and illustrated "open and go" lessons that make your job easy and stress-free!

It may be helpful to note, though, that there is often a small amount of physical prep-work needed for the lessons. This includes cutting apart the flashcards, prepping the game, or grabbing the glue for your child. What you don't need to do is struggle to understand the lesson, then repeat it in first-grader-friendly terms. That's already done for you!

The now full-color student activity books provide the meat of the lessons. Your child will be feeding words to the anteater, reading practice sentences, opening and closing the door to symbolize open and closed syllables, and so much more.

You'll also be using two phonetic readers this year. Frankly, these are the best readers we have ever seen — beautifully illustrated hardcover books with finely detailed, full-color drawings; easily advancing text; and ever-so-funny-to-first-graders storylines. From Fox's stunts in the first chapter, to the overenthusiastic work of Rawhide the ranch dog, both parents and children will enjoy the funny, wholesome stories and illustrations.

All About Reading Level 2 picks up from where your student left off in Level 1, adding new skills systematically. Many hands-on activities continue to make learning and review engaging for students, while the 27 decodable

short stories with comprehension activities take Level 2 above and beyond.

There is a convenient pretest in the beginning of the teacher's manual to make sure your child is at the most appropriate grade level. If this is your first year homeschooling and you find you need to start with an earlier level, please don't be discouraged. The results you'll get from going back and starting where he actually needs to be will be so worth the time spent!

What About the App?

While physical letter tiles are included in our standard kits, some busy families will find the continual sifting, sorting, and setup to be a bit overwhelming. That's why we suggest that you consider using the app, which does all of that for you.

Just select the lesson you are currently teaching and the appropriate letter tiles for that lesson will appear in their proper configuration, making it easy for you to teach and easy for your child to learn.

Look for the Letter Tiles app, available separately on Google Play, in Apple's App Store, and in the Kindle app store.

Scheduling

There are 54 lessons in all, so conventional scheduling would lead you to believe that completing 1.5 lessons a week is best. However, All About Reading strongly encourages you to pace yourself to the child, not the program. Isn't that a relief? They suggest simply completing 20 minutes of All About Reading time each day, knowing that some days lessons will fly by, and other days you'll want to spend more time on a concept.

SPELLING YOU SEE

BASIC ~ COMPLETE ~ ELITE

This multisensory spelling program will help your child become a confident, successful speller, naturally and at his own speed. Because Spelling You See encourages visual memory rather than rote memory, there are no weekly spelling lists or tests and very little instructor preparation. The daily lessons in Spelling You See: Jack and Jill use real words presented in context within nursery rhymes.

Spelling You See: Jack and Jill is colorful, short, to the point, and fun!

You may notice that this is your only handwriting course this year. While the publisher would advocate adding a separate workbook for handwriting, we feel that most first-graders are best served by expecting minimal writing at this stage. Your child is still developing his fine motor skills and his attention span, and allowing those skills to develop naturally will be much more appealing to both of you!

Scheduling
The 36 weeks of work, with five daily activities each week, are already planned out for you. Just open and go!

NOTE:
Never spend more than 10 minutes on spelling in a day. There is enough work in each lesson to keep a speedy writer busy for the whole 10 minutes, but a more methodical writer would be overwhelmed trying to complete it all. We highly encourage you to start a timer when you begin the day's work and stop where you are when it rings. The next day, just move on to the new lesson.

DAILY 6-TRAIT WRITING

BASIC ~ COMPLETE ~ ELITE

Are you familiar with trait writing? Trait-based writing is an impressive method educators have developed to determine whether a child's writing is skilled or not.

The six traits or characteristics that shape quality writing are content; organization; word choice; sentence fluency; voice; and conventions, which include grammar, spelling, and mechanics. It may sound ominous, but Daily 6-Trait Writing has made it effortless.

These short daily assignments are designed to build skills without being overwhelming. We love them for their brevity, but also because they are so thorough!

Scheduling

Includes 25 weeks of work which we suggest implementing as one short lesson a day, beginning on week 12 of school.

We suggest you begin when your student is ready—if you start later in the year, you'll find that the "extra" pages make great review in the summer to keep his brain sharp.

If you have a student who struggles with fine motor skills, you may have more success if you completely separate writing skills from motor skills. Most families do this by allowing their students to dictate their writing, but you could also use a whiteboard (bigger writing may be easier) or allow your student to use a computer or tablet/phone. That enables your child to build fantastic writing skills, even while his motor skills are still developing.

IMAGIDICE

~~BASIC ~~ **COMPLETE ~ ELITE**

For over 15 years, educators have been using the creative, noncompetitive Imagidice as a storytelling resource to develop students' vocabulary, imagination, and creative problem-solving skills. Each sturdy cube has six images or icons, for a total of 72 unique images. Roll some or all of the 12 Imagidice to generate a random combination of images. Then, use those images as part of your narrative.

Telling stories out loud will encourage your child to be as creative as possible without the burden of writing, spelling, and punctuation. But that only scratches the surface of the potential of what Imagidice can do. Bring Imagidice out at parties to break the ice. Use them to fine-tune foreign language abilities. Or develop expressive (putting thoughts into words) and receptive (understanding what others say) language skills in your children in a fun way with Imagidice.

You can keep it simple by rolling just one cube and asking your child to say one thing about what he sees. Or, make it much more difficult by including multiple dice and asking your child to describe what the pictures have in common. Add or swap cubes and arrive at different answers, using any aspect of the images.

The meanings of each icon on Imagidice are intentionally left open-ended to trigger multiple associations. For example, the open-mouthed person could be yelling with road rage or straining to hit the high notes of the National Anthem. That is the beauty of the ambiguity; it compels your brain to search through memories and experiences to find a meaningful association.

The icons which appear on each side of the Imagidice cubes are etched and then painted, adding to their durability.

Note: Families who do not wish to include a ghost or witch in their stories may want to remove one of the 12 dice out of their set.

Scheduling

The possibilities are truly endless with this game. We suggest breaking it out at least once a week. Looking for a new way to play? Try one of the myriad ideas online or our top 11 ideas on pages 92–93!

HANDS-ON MATH

Basic math is a critical skill for your child to master, whether he grows up to be a carpenter, doctor, accountant, or farmer. But all too often math programs rely on memorization instead of comprehension, leaving the student at a disadvantage.

That's not going to happen to your child! The real-world math problems posed in Math-U-See (combined with the hands-on manipulatives) create an unbeatable first–grade math program.

The Math-U-See manipulatives are a versatile workhorse. Not only are they integral to the curriculum, they also facilitate a depth of mathematical awareness in freeplay and fun, experimental activities.

Begin by having your child sequence the Math-U-See manipulative blocks from the shortest to the longest. Because of their precise etched segments, the manipulatives can also be used to guess and measure common items around the house. Or build a corral for those toy horses and chat about perimeter.

By using the Math-U-See manipulative blocks, your child will more easily grasp that a 1-unit block plus a 9-unit block equals a 10-unit block, and that's before you even crack open the textbooks!

MATH-U-SEE

BASIC ~ COMPLETE ~ ELITE

Math-U-See will take your child beyond mere rote memorization by using step-by-step problem solving until your child is able to reason his way through the mathematical problem. Concepts are mastered, not spiraled, to ensure greater comprehension.

Unlike some other math programs, Math-U-See does require a fair amount of parental involvement which at first glance can seem overwhelming. But they have bent over backwards to make the lesson planning as painless as possible. Better yet, at this grade feel free to merely skim the teacher's guide, as it is pretty straightforward.

The Math-U-See supplemental DVD (and teacher's guide, when you wish to use it) will teach you, the parent, more than just how to solve a math problem. It will also show why the problem is solved in this manner and when to apply the concept. DVDs can be played on a DVD player or computer; however, Windows 10 users will need to download a separate video player.

Some parents prefer to watch the lessons themselves and then teach their students personally, while most prefer to watch alongside their students, pausing the video, rewinding, or clarifying as needed.

After watching the video

lesson or your recreated lesson, your student can practice the concept for three pages, review the new concept alongside cumulative older concepts, and finally complete a "test" page to show that he has mastered the knowledge and is ready for the next week's lesson.

Your child may not need to complete every one of these pages. At the risk of oversimplifying, the practice worksheets (A, B, C) are to be used with the manipulatives until your child reaches an "aha!" moment and grasps the lesson. He may then move to the review pages (D, E, F) and should at least complete worksheet D in its entirety. If he's breezing through the pages you have a several great options. One would be to have him do every other problem, or he could skip E or F or both. (You do want to be sure he's not rusty on any of those problems before skipping, though—many students will do best completing all or most of the worksheets.) Worksheet G is often a test, application question, or extra-credit work. It's okay to skip, but valuable to complete.

Scheduling

Plan on one lesson a week, with up to seven double-sided worksheets, to complete this in a school year. That builds in a buffer of six weeks so that if your child needs a slower pace or if illness or vacations necessitate time off, you will still finish on schedule.

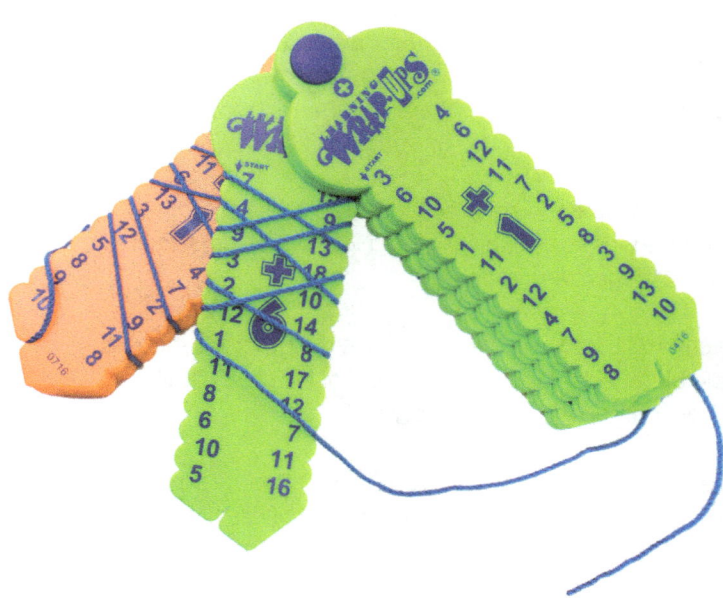

Even though math should never be just drill, it is a rare child who would not benefit from some drill work to increase speed.

Your children use Wrap-ups in the car, at the beach, at the doctor's office, or even during a home-school meeting; the possibilities are endless! Because of the portability of Wrap-ups, they can be practiced anywhere. Wrap-ups are excellent for drill-work. Challenge your child to complete a board in less than a minute before he starts the next board.

The first few times your child uses Wrap-ups you'll want to plan on some coaching. The string wraps around from the problem on the left to the answer on the right, and the motor planning involved can take a few weeks before your child really becomes fluent at that.

If the answers are correct, the string will cover the lines on the back of the board.

This is a wonderful tool for visual and kinesthetic children, and if you encourage them to say the problems aloud, it is equally marvelous for auditory children. Because it is self-correcting, your children will have immediate feedback for checking accuracy (plus, it takes you out of the picture as the bearer of "bad news").

Scheduling

Start using these Wrap-ups after your child has learned the concepts of addition and subtraction. We suggest getting these out at least once a week until he has mastered both sets.

MÖBI KIDS

~~BASIC~~ ~~COMPLETE~~ **ELITE**

Are you as tired of math drill as your children are? Then introduce your little ones to Möbi Kids, a fun, simple, and multicolored math game. Sturdy purple and green number tiles and blue double-sided operations tiles are joined by four "wild" tiles that can represent any number between 0 and 10.

Open your whale and sort the tiles by color. The blue operations tiles go within easy reach of both players. Each of you will use them as needed.

One child will use the green tiles while the other player uses purple tiles. Each child races to use all of his tiles to build number sentences crossword-style.

Primarily designed for two players, instructions are included for adapting Möbi Kids for three or more children.

Möbi Kids is an enjoyable tile game that will motivate your children to review addition and subtraction facts.

Perfect for on-the-go families, all you need to play is Möbi Kids and a flat surface.

Scheduling
Unlimited - we suggest breaking it out once a week this year.

Pro Tip
If your child isn't ready to compete (or you just can't even do one more game today!) this also makes a great solitaire

project. Once he's mastered using one set of tiles, challenge him to make a giant "crossword" that uses all of the purple and green tiles at once as shown below.

THIS IS AS CRITICAL AS IT IS APPEALING

In Timberdoodle's curriculum kits, you will find a rigorous pursuit of thinking skills for every child, in every grade. This is simply not an optional skill for your child. A child who can think logically will be able to learn well and teach himself logically in ways that an untrained brain will find difficult.

Be thankful that you won't have to persuade your child to learn to think, though – he's wired for problem solving and has been learning from the moment his eyes first saw you. We're guessing this portion of the curriculum will be the hardest not to race through. After all, who doesn't want to use tiles to solve a problem, arrange the cookies correctly on the cookie sheet, or be the fastest to deliver the mail to the right house?

CRITICAL & CREATIVE

BASIC ~ COMPLETE ~ ELITE

The relationship between critical and creative thought can be misunderstood. But in fact, profound thinking requires both imagination and intellectual ideas. To produce excellence in thinking, we need to engage our children in a curriculum that overlaps the logical and the imaginative sides of thinking.

Critical & Creative's 46 theme-based units will give your child lots of practice thinking in a variety of ways. From brainteasers and logic puzzles to mazes, Venn diagrams, and secret codes, Critical & Creative Thinking Activities has a wealth of mind-boggling activities that your child will enjoy while he learns thinking fluency, originality, generalizing, patterning, and problem solving.

One important note: This is not a handwriting course! We feel that most first-graders will be overwhelmed if you expect them to write out all of their answers this year. Instead, we encourage you to sit down with your child and jot down his answers as dictated to you. The lessons are short, and this will keep interest to a maximum and tedium to a minimum.

Scheduling
With 142 pages in all, we suggest simply doing four pages a week. Or if you'd rather work by units just complete 1–2 a week.

FYI, while we find Critical & Creative to be a very valuable series, it is published by a secular publisher, and our conservative family would at the very least have skipped pages 17–19.

Most children naturally gravitate to hands-on activities. Why not harness that inclination with a hands-on thinking skills program? miniLUK is used around the world for teaching/reviewing thinking skills concepts, math, visual perception, and so much more!

Complete kits include a miniLUK board & sampler book, along with seven complete books of puzzles to solve, focusing on critical thinking and visual perception skills. If you opted for the Elite Curriculum Package, you also received 13 additional puzzle books. Make sure you reserve the advanced sets for use after your child has completed the rest of the books. They increase in difficulty as he goes, and you won't want him to jump ahead and get discouraged.

Scheduling

We suggest doing four new puzzle pages a week and as many review pages as your child would like. (Or, if you purchased the Elite kit, he can complete seven to eight new puzzles every week.)

Note: miniLUK is amazingly easy to play once you've seen it in action. So, if the package directions seem confusing, just visit www.Timberdoodle.com/miniLUK for a quick video demo.

SMART COOKIES

~~BASIC~~ **COMPLETE ~ ELITE**

Using visual clues and some fundamental logic principles, your child will be asked to place Smart Cookies' nine delectable treats on the tray. New concepts are introduced in a measured manner, with each additional snack-sized concept requiring your child to use more complex reasoning skills. As he progresses through eight levels of deductive logic, he will develop and strengthen his reasoning skills while advancing at his own pace.

Scheduling

Smart Cookies comes with 64 puzzles to solve, so doing just two a week will complete the course this year.

POSTMAN OBSERVATION GAME

~~BASIC~~ ~~COMPLETE~~ **ELITE**

Imported from Spain, Postman Observation Game will test your child's visual acuity as well as his visual memory and ability to respond quickly. To begin, your child assembles the city in any configuration he wishes. Then, as each card is turned over, he rushes to locate the matching building among the nearly 90 that are shown. The first one to find the right structure places one of his letter tokens on it, and the first to deliver all of his letters wins.

For an additional challenge, there are harder levels of play. Some cards will ask you to find one or more houses based on a detailed description, and other cards will ask you to find a storybook character's home. These more difficult quests make Postman a multigenerational game that will grow with your family.

And because you can set up the city differently every time you play, Postman stays fresh and entertaining! A beautiful game, Postman is for two to six players, ages three and up.

Scheduling
As with the rest of the games in your kit, we suggest pulling this out at least once a week and doing as many rounds as you'd like.

HOW DID A 6-YEAR-OLD BECOME THE LAST EMPEROR OF ROME?

Many history curriculum options make the mistake of focusing solely on U.S.A. history. As important as that is, doesn't it make more sense to start with the big picture of history? This year you'll learn about ancient times, covering the major historical events in the years 5000 B.C. – A.D. 400, from the early nomads to the last Roman emperor. You'll answer questions like:

What terrible secret was buried in Shi Huangdi's tomb?
Did nomads like lizard stew?
What happened to Anansi the Spider in the Village of the Plantains?
And, of course, how did a 6-year-old become the last emperor of Rome?

You'll supplement the ancient geography in The Story of the World with the vibrant pages of Skill Sharpeners Geography to master important geography concepts. You'll get to do all of this while scrutinizing a scrunchable, packable, nearly-indestructible map.

STORY OF THE WORLD

~~BASIC~~ **COMPLETE ~ ELITE**

This is very easy to use. Just read your child one chapter from the story book, then ask him to tell you what it was about. Afterward, pick an activity page or worksheet that is appropriate for your child's interest and your schedule.

Some first-graders will initially have trouble staying tuned in for Story of the World. If that's your child, check out the auditory processing tips on pages 72–73.

Did you see how big the activity book is? Keep in mind that one of its biggest advantages is the fact that it offers a wide range of activities for each lesson. Pick the ones that best fit your child's learning style and your family's schedule, but don't try to do them all!

Scheduling

Completing three chapters every two weeks is a realistic pace that will get you through the books in just under a year. If you purchased the Elite kit, you'll love having the audio book. It includes the same content as the story book, but it can be much more convenient. Just pop in the CD and listen to your history with your child while you're driving, cooking, feeding the baby, or any of the myriad other activities that keep your hands too busy to hold a book.

Note: Please do not consider this series a Providential view of history which recognizes God's hand in history, but rather a history text that attempts to include all significant historical and cultural accounts. Where you find details with Biblical references that are inaccurate because of sparseness, use this opportunity to interject more of His story. Simply skip anything that is uncomfortable for your family. These are very minor issues that are easily addressed and shouldn't keep you from this overall excellent program.

SKILL SHARPENERS GEOGRAPHY

~~BASIC~~ **COMPLETE ~ ELITE**

Skill Sharpeners Geography lets your child explore his world while learning key map skills and geography concepts with little fuss on your part. The cross-curricular activities integrate the most current geography standards, and each eye-catching book is divided into colorful collections of engaging, grade-appropriate themes.

Each theme includes short nonfiction reading selections, comprehension questions, vocabulary practice, and writing prompts.

Optional hands-on activities will excite the kinesthetic child in your home. To use them you'll need a few common tools, like scissors, glue, tape, and coloring materials. It may also be helpful to note that there are a couple of activities (pages 69 and 79 in Skill Sharpeners Geography) which suggest that you first glue the pieces together and then color the scene. In our opinion, it would at least be worth considering whether to have your child color first and then cut those pieces out. For some kids, that would be less frustrating than coloring on top of glued paper.

Skill Sharpeners Geography takes your child beyond just the basics of geography and includes a smattering of histories and cultures within our world. The colorful illustrations and pages will grab your child's attention, and the handy

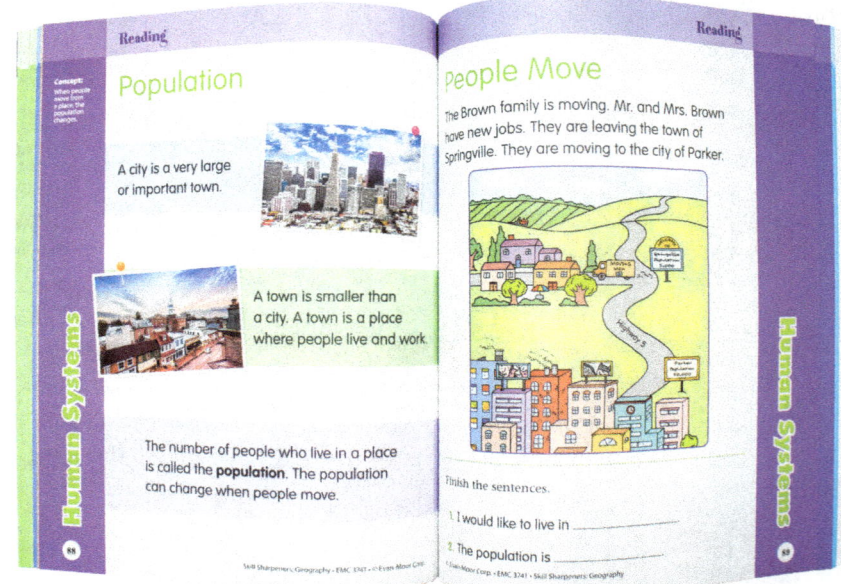

(removable) answer key in the back allows you to help your student to easily check his work.

Scheduling

Instead of going by actual page count (135), it makes more sense to split up the work by activity pages. So each week you'll want to complete any instructional pages needed as well as about two activities.

And yes, you may truly skip the activity pages (with no guilt) if that isn't how your child learns best. In that case, plan on four pages a week, including the skipped activity pages.

SCRUNCHMAP WORLD

What an ideal tool for a first-grader! His ScrunchMap is both convenient and portable. Printed onto water- and tear-resistant material, ScrunchMaps are as kid-proof as you can get. So take your ScrunchMap out to the tree house, down to the beach, up the mountain, and across the country; this map is designed to be a workhorse.

ScrunchMap is a great reference tool. In addition, here are some ways to use ScrunchMap to build geography skills:

Find the modern-day equivalent to where your last ancient history lesson was based.

What countries form your family heritage? Point them out to your child.

Where have you visited, and where have your child's friends traveled?

Show your child the countries where far-flung friends or acquaintances live.

Find the country where an item you use was manufactured.

Where were your fruits and veggies grown, or what countries are they native to?

Have you eaten any cultural foods, such as sushi, curry, or gelato? Find the countries they originate from.

Do you have a German shepherd or a Portuguese water dog? Talk about where your pet or dream pet originated.

Does your church support missionaries, or do you sponsor a child? How about church plants? Where are they located?

What news story could you discuss with your child, pointing out the location of the event?

Scheduling

Unlimited. A good goal would be to utilize the ScrunchMap World at least once a week.

FAMOUS FIGURES

~~BASIC~~ ~~COMPLETE~~ **ELITE**

With Famous Figures of Ancient Times, you'll find that history becomes hands-on as you assemble movable figures of 21 of the key characters of old, from King David to Jesus, and from Emperor Qin Shi Huangdi to Julius Caesar. While listening to The Story of the World, your avid artist can color in the detailed figures. A hole punch and common fasteners will allow their arms and legs to move and their swords and shields to flash. For the meticulous child who wants to color it exactly right, matching pre-colored action figures are also included.

Scheduling

Aim to do a figure every week or two, or time them to match up with Story of the World as follows.

1. Narmer: Chapter 2
2. *Khufu: Chapter 4
3. Sargon the Great: Chapters 5–6
4. Hammurabi: Chapters 7–8
5. Hatshepsut: Chapter 13
6. Moses: Chapter 14
7. *David: Chapter 15
8. Ashurbanipal: Chapter 16
9. Nebuchadnezzar II: Chapter 17
10. Cyrus the Great: Chapters 21–22
11. *Aristotle: Chapter 22
12. A Greek Hoplite (foot soldier): Chapters 22–24
13. Alexander the Great: Chapter 25
14. Hannibal: Chapter 29
15. Hannibal's War Elephant: Chapter 29
16. Qin Shi Huangdi: Chapter 32
17. Julius Caesar: Chapter 34
18. Caesar Augustus: Chapters 36 & 37
19. Jesus: Chapter 37
20. Constantine the Great: Chapter 39
21. *Augustine: Chapter 41

*FYI this person is not directly spoken of in the chapter but is part of this era.

READY TO EXPERIMENT?

The Berean Science series teaches science as discovered throughout history, so it makes perfect sense for the series to open right at the beginning with the six days of creation. Science in the Beginning provides 15 lessons for each of the six days of creation, incorporating a vast variety of topics and experiments.

These include light and eyesight in Unit 1; tornadoes in Unit 2; a crayon rock cycle in Unit 3; a toilet paper map of the solar system in Unit 4; whether saltwater or freshwater fish drink more in Unit 5; and how cats, dogs, and rabbits see differently in Unit 6. All the while, students are referred back to the Creator who fashioned all the marvels they are studying. You're going to love this!

SCIENCE IN THE BEGINNING

~~BASIC~~ **COMPLETE ~ ELITE**

Berean Science offers students an opportunity to study science through the lens of history. Using a narrative dialogue and a Christian worldview, Berean Science teaches science chronologically, so there are vast and varied science topics in each volume.

Fairly bursting with experiments—every lesson has some sort of activity—Berean Science's strong focus on this hands-on component makes it an ideal program for the wigglers in your household.

The durable hardcover textbook has lots of full-color illustrations. The lessons are concise but complete, drilling down to the core of what your child needs to know. Lesson material is often just a page or two following each activity, perfect for any child that struggles to sit and pay attention. (If that's a struggle, though, don't worry–see pages 72–73 for tips on making strides.)

The activities, all color-coded and easy to find quickly, often involve inexpensive household items and are the gateway to the exploration of each scientific concept. Plus, each book has a helpful section in the front that tells you all the materials you will need, broken down per chapter, for doing the experiments.

Each lesson concludes with questions or additional activities for "younger," "older," and "oldest" students, so Berean Science lends itself well to multi-grade homes that prefer to use just one science curriculum for the entire family.

Lessons are taught directly from the text, so there is no cumbersome teacher's manual.

If your student appreciates beginning with notebooking pages rather than a blank notebook, check out the free PDFs from the publisher on our website.

Scheduling

You'll notice that some of the lessons in your book are red in the table of contents. A red lesson indicates that this lesson is optional–a bonus lesson, if you will.

If you wish to only complete essential lessons, just do two lessons a week. However, if you prefer to enjoy every single lesson, you'll want to do two to three lessons a week. (In fact, if you alternate between two and three lessons, you'll come out exactly on track.)

Pro Tip:

The most intimidating part of science can be gathering the supplies required for experiments. If you purchased the Elite kit, take advantage of the lab kit included. If not, we recommend you stop now, grab a box and the list of materials printed in the introductory pages of your textbook, and collect all your needed materials, purchasing any items you need for the year on your next shopping trip. Make it more fun by considering it a full-family scavenger hunt!

Besides everyday dishware and perishable items, you should be able to collect most other items you need, and you'll never regret having already completed the most labor-intensive step of your child's science education this year.

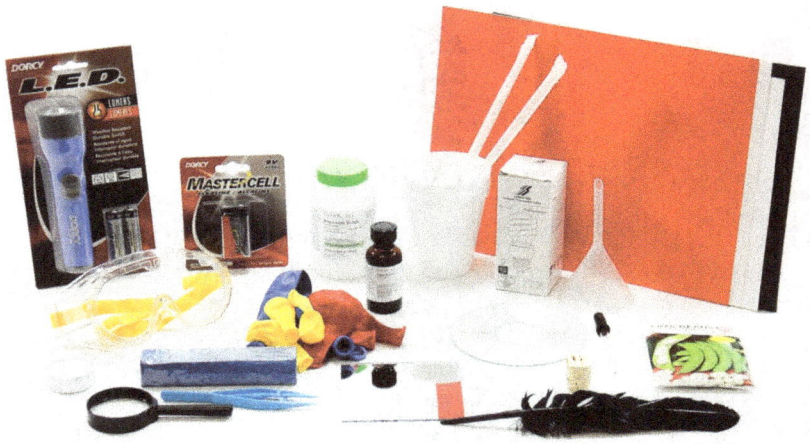

STEM IS EVERYWHERE!

STEM learning is more than robotics and computer programming. STEM tools also include those that engage students in exploratory learning, discovery, and problem solving and that teach the foundational skills of critical thinking and short- and long-term planning. So STEM includes your What's New? What's Missing? What's Different? book as well as your Smart Cookies logic game and your Aquarellum Cosmos set. Basically anything that goes beyond a rote read-and-regurgitate lesson undoubtedly falls into the STEM classification. In assembling this guide, many of our products could easily have been classified as STEM, but these two sets seem especially appropriate for this category.

PLUS-PLUS 1200 WITH BASEPLATE

~~BASIC~~ **COMPLETE ~ ELITE**

Hand your child Plus-Plus and he will intuitively begin to create. Plus-Plus' identical simple shapes with their slightly rubbery texture glide smoothly together with very little pressure, and they stay together!

One of the unique things about this kit is that you can choose to make remarkable flat mosaics or impressive 3D models. You will be astonished at what your first-grader comes up with.

Plus-Plus encourages children to think creatively about color, design, and structure and is a painless way to develop fine motor skills and hand-eye coordination.

Plus-Plus has gained a tremendous following over the last few years in Denmark where it is used in schools. At the back of this first-grade handbook is the exclusive Timberdoodle Plus-Plus Guide for Parents. In it you will find 36 weeks of Plus-Plus ideas for your child and 36 models to inspire creativity.

Timberdoodle's custom Plus-Plus set includes a baseplate that we've found to be helpful for intricate or free-standing designs.

Scheduling
You're going to want to have your child building every week. Start by using the 36-week program that begins on page 100.

If your child finds moving from flat construction to 3-D models challenging, or if he simply wants more ideas, look at the extra instructions on page 127 and following.

Plus-Plus makes a great fidget while he listens to history or science, so if you need more ideas why not have him build something from today's other studies? Perhaps a cookie, a word, a figure from history... We'd love to see your child's models if you would care to share them with us on Facebook!

ROBOTIS PETS

~~BASIC~~ ~~COMPLETE~~ **ELITE**

Robotis Pets features step-by-step assembly instructions which show your child how to build a variety of pets with different mechanized actions. This introduces your child to the fundamentals of simple automation. Robotis Pets is easy to assemble, so imaginative scientists can expand on these ideas while exercising creativity and developing fine motor skills. What a great combination for learning science, technology, engineering, and math concepts. You will need to provide two AA batteries.

For a child that is new to construction, it will help if you work with him to gather all the parts before he begins construction. As he becomes more experienced at assembling his robots, you'll probably find he naturally invents his own. Did he come up with a new animal? We want to know!

Scheduling

Assemble a robotic pet every month. There are three ideas given in the booklet, and four others are available on the Robotis app (R+ Design: available for smart phones and PCs). Towards the end of the school year, challenge your child to build a robot every month from memory.

STEM OR STEAM?

STEM, an acronym for Science, Technology, Engineering, and Mathematics, has recently been joined by Art to form STEAM. Is it really that important? Yes! Art is used to plan the layout of a tower, the design of a prosthetic hand, and the colors of the latest app. In fact, as long as your project is inquiry-based and you have the opportunity to think critically, creatively, and innovatively, then you are looking at a STEAM curriculum. Because the transition of terminology from STEM to STEAM is still tentative, we are using STEM for clarity's sake and listing art here separately in this handbook. But don't let that fool you into overlooking art this year. It really is a vital skill!

WHAT'S NEW? WHAT'S MISSING...

BASIC ~ COMPLETE ~ ELITE

Children love to learn and love to create. What's New? What's Missing? What's Different? combines those two delights into one sure-to-please workbook for early learners.

From drawing different pillows under napping cats, to finding the unusual flamingos in the flock, even completing the missing parts of dogs, What's New? What's Missing? What's Different? inspires your young learners to discern both broad and subtle differences and respond creatively. What's New? What's Missing? What's Different? will strengthen your child's focus and attention to detail in an engaging, mind-stretching manner.

We were disappointed when this title went out of print a few years ago, so we are very excited to be bringing it back as a

Timberdoodle Exclusive this year. You and your child will love this!

Scheduling

There are 42 spreads included, each requiring varying amounts of work. We'd suggest completing 1–2 spreads a week. Consider breaking that up over multiple days as some of the pages have a lot of different drawing or thinking activities crammed onto them. Regardless of how fun they are, that could be overwhelming for a first-grader to do in one sitting, but much more fun to do a little each day.

Note: If you're as picky as we are, a couple of the pages in What's New? What's Missing? What's Different? will not appeal to you. Overall, however, we found this to be such an excellent book that we couldn't resist offering it to you.

Your student will learn how to mix rich, vibrant colors while he creates beautiful and detailed works of art. With Aquarellum's exclusive water-resistant technique, paint flows off the wax barriers and adheres only to the design motif areas, making the vivid colors pop. Aquarellum's color-mixing guide shows how to blend a variety of colors.

There are many methods to choose from. Painting quickly prevents uneven water patterns; painting slowly achieves a characteristic watercolor look. Your child can add layers of increasingly dark tints until he reaches the desired result, or he can mix paints in the palette to create just the right hue, even adding water to lighten a color's shade.

Aquarellum Cosmos is a genius way to exponentially increase your child's color-mixing and design skills, while the water-resistant technique allows even novices to create beautiful artwork.

Scheduling

There are two "canvases" in this set. If you're up to setting up a watercolor station each week, it would be ideal to work on it for 20 minutes at a time and then let it dry and continue the next week. If that's not feasible (toddlers, anyone?), consider saving the kit for holidays when your child needs a time-absorbing, relaxing activity that can also double as a handmade gift for loved ones.

DOODLE WASHINGTON D.C.

~~BASIC~~ ~ **COMPLETE ~ ELITE**

Some years ago the top buzzword for business was "creative." A few years later, the hot topic in education became creativity.

This trickle-down development should spur educators, especially those of us teaching at home, to look beyond easy "read-and-regurgitate" education that dulls the mind. Instead, we should lead a lifestyle that not only encourages imaginative efforts, but that also passionately carves out time for those pursuits every day.

The finest method we have found is both surprisingly easy and affordable – doodle books. A doodle a day has the potential of engaging both sides of the brain and unleashing a powerhouse of originality. And, with so much variety, it never gets old.

Draw colorful flags in front of the embassies, doodle a sculpture for the National Gallery Sculpture Garden, draw plants for the Botanic Garden, and put lights on the National Christmas Tree.

With these prompts and many more, Doodle Washington D.C. will encourage your child to imagine life in the U.S. national capital. Some doodles are specific to Washington D.C., such as doodling a horse for General Grant's statue, while others are universally fun, like decorating the cupcakes with lots of colors. But all of the doodles will inspire your child's creativity and imagination.

Scheduling
With 95 doodles to complete, you'll want to plan on 2-3 a week in order to finish this year.

Note: Doodle Washington D.C. is refreshingly innocent and child-friendly. However, families who do not celebrate Halloween may prefer to skip a page or two.

COSMOS FOIL

~~BASIC~~ ~~COMPLETE~~ **ELITE**

Djeco's Cosmos Foil is a super-fun craft project for your first-grader. Using an innovative two-step process, Cosmos Foil is versatile, sparkly, and mess-free! Your child first chooses and adheres a space-themed adhesive shape to one of the included beautifully illustrated artboards, or to his own notebook or craft project. He then rubs the dazzling metallic foil on the sticker for a stunning effect!

Cosmos Foil comes in a little folder for secure storage and travel. It contains eight sheets of space-themed stickers, 10 sheets of impressive metallic foil, and 12 space scene cards to decorate. Cosmos Foil provides your child with a unique, flashy way to be creative.

Scheduling

With 12 cards to decorate, you could have your child do one every three weeks and finish up on time. Or just break them out as desired to brighten up a dull week.

Do Art Coloring with Clay

~~BASIC~~ ~~COMPLETE~~ **ELITE**

Do Art Coloring with Clay is a brilliant clay coloring kit that uses pre-printed boards for children to create amazing, eye-popping works of art. Color in areas by pinching off small amounts of clay and pressing them on. Tiny clay balls can be flattened to make the suction pad of a tree frog, clay rods can be used to fill in larger areas like the lion's mane. Your child can marbleize, layer, and blend the 12 vibrant clay colors to create one-of-a-kind masterpieces.

A special rubber-tip tool makes blending a snap, and the three double-sided clay tools allow your child to experiment with textures. Do Art Coloring with Clay will guide your child through the creation of the four amusing animal designs with a remarkably helpful color booklet. Do Art Coloring with Clay includes everything your child will need to complete these treasured works of art.

Scheduling

With four projects to complete, your child can work on them bit by bit every month or finish an entire craft as a wonderful afternoon project.

LET THEM WIGGLE!

When one of our children was a preschooler, we received the best advice a parent of a kinesthetic child could receive: Let her wiggle. And wiggle she did. I don't think she sat for schoolwork for many years, but she learned! The negative? Pirouettes and somersaults can be a huge distraction to a child's siblings.

A workable compromise is a handheld fidget like Mad Mattr that lets your child work his muscles and keep his brain active without him whirling around the room!

The other learning tool in this section is a test prep guide that will help you and your child go into any mandatory testing with a big boost in confidence.

MAD MATTR CRAFTSMAN

~~BASIC ~~ **COMPLETE ~ ELITE**

A Swedish phenomenon that has swept throughout Europe like wildfire is now available in the US! Mad Mattr, an amazingly moldable, stretchable, dough-like compound, can be shaped into countless brilliantly colored creations. Silky to the touch, Mad Mattr never dries out – ever.

Wheat-, gluten-, casein-, and odor-free, Mad Mattr is firm to the touch, but it will quickly loosen to be soft, airy, and malleable. Pressed against a textured surface, Mad Mattr makes a stunningly accurate imprint. Or pull it apart gently and it will stream into a puddle on your table.

Unleash your child's creative side without destroying your home with Mad Mattr. Virtually mess-free, it doesn't stain and won't stick to your carpet, furniture, clothes, or books. And the bits and pieces that materialize on your work surface are easily gathered, sticking to one another and not to the table.

In fact, it is for that very reason that we've included Mad Mattr as a learning tool this year. It packs all the benefits of Thinking Putty as a fidget, but without the mess or potential for household damage!

In Craftsman, you have not only the ability to create building bricks that lock together, but there are also six shaped extruders and a safe cutting tool to create cookies, pillars, and jewels.

Scheduling

There really are unlimited ways to use this tool. Its primary purpose is that of a fidget, perfect for your child to play with while he watches his math lessons or at other times when his mind is more engaged than his hands. Are you looking for specific things to do with Mad Mattr? Check out pages 92–99 for 52 different ideas to liven up your Mad Mattr time each week. (Some first-graders will have outgrown these ideas, while others will relish them. Try them with your child and see what he thinks!)

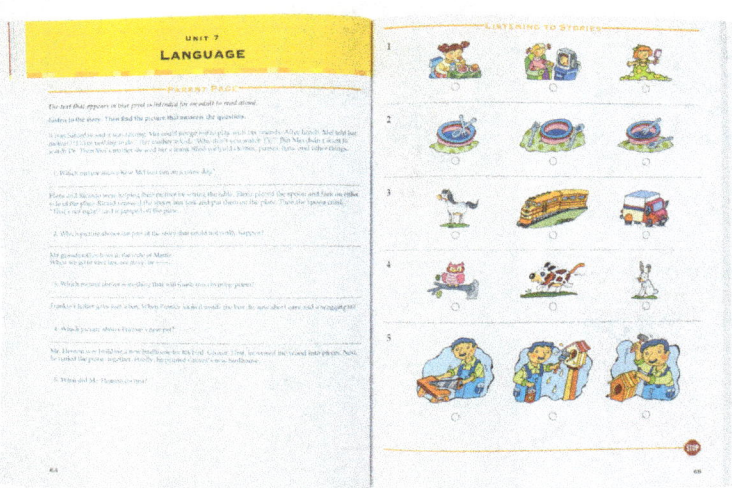

may continue to home educate. Why not make sure your children are "playing on a level playing field?" The Test Prep series offers students the essential groundwork needed to prepare for standardized tests.

Based on subject areas covered by most state standardized tests, these colorful, inviting workbooks provide a good sampling of all the skills required of each grade level. Practice pages, strategies, tips, and full-length practice tests build test-taking confidence and skills in subjects such as reading comprehension, vocabulary, language, and math. The test tips are beneficial, and the information and instructions are super-easy to follow. Developed by a leading educational publisher, Harcourt's Test Prep provides a great opportunity for children to review before taking standardized state tests. Engaging, practical, and easy to use, Test Prep will help your children face the tests with the same confidence that their peers will have.

Even if your state doesn't require testing, consider completing the book anyway, since test-taking skills are vital across all areas of life.

Scheduling
Our family has always preferred to spend the week or two before our state-mandated annual testing working through this book. Keep it low key, and let the change of pace be an enjoyable experience for your child. If you run into a concept he doesn't know, stop and explain it to him; that is why you are doing the prep now!

Home-taught children who are not prepared for their yearly standardized tests are at a distinct disadvantage to the government- and privately-taught children. If you reside in a state that requires standardized tests, you should know that a vast majority of certified teachers teach with the test in mind. In other words, teachers understand the types of questions that will appear on the standardized tests, and they will spend weeks preceding the tests covering the necessary information. If you do not do likewise, your children stand a chance of performing poorly in comparison.

For those of us in a state where some form of testing is required, but never scrutinized, preparing is not as critical. But some of you are in states where the test results are not only analyzed but are used as a basis for whether you

FROM OUR FAMILY TO YOURS

In 1986, we were a family of five. I was the oldest of three toddler girls with a mom who absolutely excelled at educating us at home. Of course, this was during "The Dark Ages" of homeschooling, and online searching was still a thing of the future. Our mom, Deb, was (and is) a voracious reader, though, and an avid researcher. We girls were thriving academically and, naturally, other moms were interested in using the same curricula Deb had found.

So, in 1986 she and Dan, our dad, repurposed the business license originally intended for their world-class Golden Retriever breeding operation (which had come to naught) and she launched Timberdoodle, a homeschool supply company. A catalog was born, and growth came fast. We shipped from our laundry room, the grandparents' basement, and finally, warehouses and an office. Two more children were added, and all of us grew up working in the business from an early age.

Now, decades later, Timberdoodle is still renowned for out-of-the-box learning and crazy-smart finds. Mom's engineering background has heavily influenced our STEM selections, and her no-nonsense, independent approach has made these kits the award-winning choice that they are today.

All five of us are grown now, and most still work at Timberdoodle in key roles. Our brother and his wife have welcomed sweet new babies, and we sisters have opened our home to children through foster care and adoption. As our families have grown, we've become even more committed to equipping parents with the best homeschooling resources. The kits we sell are the same ones we use in our own homes, and we hope you enjoy them as much as we do.

In the following articles, you'll hear from Deb and others about some of the nitty-gritty questions we often field. Do you have a question not answered here? Don't forget that you are invited to contact us at any time—we'd love to help!

Joy (for all of us)

MY FIRST-GRADER CAN'T LISTEN!

HOW TO TEACH AUDITORY PROCESSING WITHOUT LOSING YOUR MIND

Timberdoodle kits are renowned for hands-on components, which means that many of you switched to Timberdoodle specifically to help your kinesthetic learner. Yay! It's perfect!

But then you find a problem. Your science and history courses this year rely on a lot of listening unless your student is reading far above his grade level. Some students will hang on every word, while for others listening for an entire chapter will be a huge challenge.

So now what? Is this a battle worth fighting? We would argue that it definitely is! As your student gets older, he will find more and more frequently that he needs to be able to take in and utilize information he receives only through his ears. (Side note: Have you ever considered that it is nearly impossible to teach history without using words? After all, there are many horrific historical moments that you want to be able to discuss, not reenact!)

If you find that your student struggles to stay focused, there are a few things to keep in mind.

First, he's not alone. Every first-grade classroom is filled with bubbly little kids whose attention splits at a moment's notice.

Science and history are introductory materials at this grade level, and they will all be revisited in more depth at a later time. So if you feel like there is information that your student isn't retaining, you're probably right, but you shouldn't find that discouraging!

Also, these courses were written for a range of grades. Some of the material is geared for the older siblings in the group, though you may be surprised by how much of that your first-grader can actually grasp with the proper training!

Now, on a practical note, getting his hands busy might help:

- You could get out the activity pages/notebooking pages first so that he can color while you read.

- Maybe he'd prefer to grab his Plus-Plus and build while he listens.

- Break out the Mad Mattr–it's in your kit particularly for such a time as this!

Now that he's set up, start reading. You want to read up until just before his attention wanders. If he's a typical first-grader, one paragraph may be the perfect amount to start with!

Read a paragraph, and then ask him what happened/ what the point was/if he thought X was actually going to work... If he can answer, set the book aside and move to whatever is his "fun part" of school. (You'll come back to the book paragraph by paragraph throughout the day.) If he struggles, read the paragraph again and give him another try at answering. As time goes by, you'll be able to read two paragraphs, then three, and more.

The beauty of this approach is that you are actively working to build his auditory processing, an essential learning skill.

If this continues to be an issue, it is never a bad idea to loop your pediatrician into the conversation. You may find that there is a physical component (such as hearing impairment) that is underlying the issue and really should be addressed.

Some kids will always be wiggly, and that is just fine. Your goal is to equip your wiggler to learn in all the ways he can, and homeschooling is ideal for that!

WHAT MAKES GAMES A PRIORITY?

6 REASONS GAMES AREN'T JUST FOR FUN, EVEN THE "FRIVOLOUS" GAMES

You may have noticed that this year there is at least one multi-player game in every curriculum kit. This is not just to add some levity to your day!

The Research

A quick google search will net you numbers of articles on the benefits of playing board games with your children. Here are just some of those benefits:

- increasing laughter
- language development
- understanding rules
- grasping fair play
- detecting patterns and predicting outcomes
- learning from experience
- impulse control

- social skills
- increasing focus
- teamwork
- reducing anxiety
- unplugging from technology
- increasing analytical abilities
- setting goals
- patience
- problem solving skills
- reducing stress
- creativity
- prioritizing steps towards a goal
- self-confidence
- spatial ability

This is a robust and interwoven list, but here are the five things that have jumped out at us over the past year and made this a huge priority for your child's education.

1. Social-Emotional Intelligence

Think of your closest and dearest friends outside of your immediate family. What makes them so dear to you? My guess is that it isn't their IQ or ability to speed-solve complex math problems. A friendship will celebrate those interesting facts, but your friendship itself is more likely rooted in shared interests, time spent, and an ability to navigate hard situations with grace.

When you spend time teaching a child how to lose graciously, you are teaching a life skill that will translate into all of life and impact their friendships way more than their test scores ever could.

In light of this, the end of each game may be more important than the strategy in the middle. Coach your children in what you expect from the winner and the loser. Around here, a "Good game!" goes a long way, but you decide what is best for your family. Humility is what you're looking to see. Not the teary deflation of a proud loser or the puffed up bragging of a proud winner!

2. Strategic Thinking

Obviously, the games we've chosen require age-appropriate logic and strategy. Critical thinking skills are essential, so let's teach them any way we may.

3. Connection

It can seem that as your children get older, your parenting gets more and more hands-off. Or, for a younger child, it may seem that you spend more time correcting behavior than you do connecting with your child. Making games a priority lets you enjoy each other's company and genuinely become closer to each other. What parent won't appreciate that?

4. Executive Functioning

Are you familiar with executive functioning? It is the ability to prioritize and organize information. The clearest example we've been given is the age-old challenge to "guess what number I'm thinking of right now using yes or no questions." If you respond by asking if the number is higher than 100, you are using executive functioning. If instead you start rattling off numbers, you're not. In games you're constantly taking into consideration what your opponent is doing, what pieces are still in your hand, which rules apply at the moment... and sorting/utilizing all the information to decide what your next game play should be.

5. Regulation

Some articles tie this to executive fuctioning, but it's worth discussing on its own. Regulation is the ability to control your own emotions - can you think of a more natural opportunity to practice this than during game play? Calm-down strategies and redos may be implemented as many times as needed, until your child is able to endure suspense and even win or lose without outbursts. Phew!

6. Growth Mindset

Yes, this is a buzzword right now, but it is worth mentioning. Some of us, students included, tend to think that we are good at something or we're not. For our PreK twins this has been particularly obvious in our discussions about art. One has a natural inclination for drawing and one does not. So the naturally gifted one calls himself an artist and proclaims that his brother is not. It is helpful to come back and discuss that we all learn and grow. So when Mr. Artist set aside his art for several months and his twin worked and worked at it, we had two artists on our hands! Gameplay is a natural place to model that all of us learn and grow in our skill sets. You aren't simply "born with it" but you learn skills and develop abilities.

Side Note: Think Out Loud

An article from Parenting Science made an excellent point that students don't always naturally ask why a player used a specific strategy. Try to start that conversation by asking why he chose to _ or explain that you're starting with this piece because _. This will model the higher-order thinking that you are setting out to teach. It will also model the fact that we are all learners here!

So what are you waiting for? Go play some games!

WHY EMPHASIZE INDEPENDENT LEARNING?

THE TOP SEVEN REASONS THIS IS SUCH A BIG DEAL AT TIMBERDOODLE

1. Avoid Burn Out

One-on-one teaching is critical to the success of any student, and homeschoolers are no exception to that. However, we have seen parents who become helicopter teachers, micromanaging every detail of their students' education. Is it any wonder that these parents burn out? Independent learning tools provide a natural transition from the one-on-one of early childhood to a less teacher-intense educational approach.

2. Cultivate Responsible Learners

There is a lot of (dare we say it?) fun in teaching. But it is better for your students if they master how to learn on their own. After all, when they are adults, you'll want them to have the ability to pick up any skill they want and learn it as needed. Structuring their education to be more and more self-taught helps them to become responsible self-learners.

3. Special Needs, Illness, and Newborns

Not all parents have the same amount of teaching time. Whether they are doing therapy for a child with autism, dealing with their own chronic illness, managing visits for a foster child, or are blessed with a newborn, there are seasons when homeschooling needs to be more independent simply for the teacher's sanity!

4. You Don't Have to Love Teaching

As much as no one wants to mention this, we all know parents who really struggle to teach. They love their kids and feel strongly about homeschooling, but when it actually comes down to teaching they are easily overwhelmed and intimidated. If it is an area they are not gifted/trained in, then of course teaching is scary. Independent learning tools can help get them comfortable in their role, but even if they never love teaching they can still reap the benefits of giving their children a superior education at home.

5. Timberdoodle's Purpose: We Are Here to Make Giving Your Children a Superior Education at Home Enjoyable

Here at Timberdoodle, amid the catalogs, sales, blog posts, videos, Facebook giveaways, etc., we have one primary goal. That goal is to make it possible for parents to enjoy giving their children a superior education at home. We aren't here to sell you stuff (though we wouldn't exist if you didn't shop!), which is why we have been known to send you to our "competitors" when their product would work better for you. We really just want you to be a happy homeschool family. When that happens, we feel successful! Independent learning is one tool in your toolbox. It is a valuable tool, so use it where it works best for you.

6. Not Either/Or

You don't have to pick between independent and group learning across the board. Take The Fallacy Detective, for instance. It is designed for a student to pick up and read independently. Instead, our family did it as a read-aloud and took turns answering the questions. The result? Not only did we have a blast, but we were also all on the same page regarding logical fallacies. Bumper stickers and ads we came across in daily life were fodder for vigorous discussions

about the underlying fallacies in ways that would never have happened if we each studied it alone. So even if you're striving to teach independent learning, don't hesitate to do some things together!

7. Our Family

The rule of thumb in our house was that as soon as a child could read, he or she was responsible for his or her own education. We each had an annual conference with Mom to set learning goals for the year, then we were given the books for the year, often including the teacher's manuals. Mom gave us each a weekly checklist to complete before Friday Family Night. If we needed help, we were to ask for it. Otherwise, the responsibility was ours. This freed us up to do the truly important things (devotions, service, Timberdoodle work, babysitting, elder care, church projects, hospitality, farming...) as a family.

10 REASONS TO STOP SCHOOL WORK AND GO BUILD SOMETHING!

Would you like to supplement your curriculum with a program that simultaneously improves your child's visual perception, fine motor skills, patience, problem solving, spatial perception, creativity, ability to follow directions, pre-reading skills, grasp of physics concepts, and engineering ability? Better yet, what if your child would actually enjoy this curriculum and choose to do it whenever he could? No, this isn't some mythical homeschool product guaranteed to solve all your problems for a large fee—we are talking about the LEGO® bricks already strewn throughout your house, the blocks in our preschool curriculum, and the Bioloid robot kit designed for teens.

Construction kits just might be the most underrated type of curriculum ever. It's not just us; research concludes that children learn a lot by designing and building things. Based on our own engineering background/bias, we believe that construction is one of the most valuable educational processes available. For that reason, both learning to build and learning by what has been built should be a part of every family's curriculum. Here are our top 10 skills your child will learn with his construction kit:

1. Visual Perception

It may be obvious that it takes visual perception to find the right pieces and place them well, but consider that whether your child is reading, finishing a puzzle, or doing open-heart surgery, a proficiency in visual perception is mandatory!

2. Fine Motor Skills

Boys especially seem to struggle with fine motor skills, particularly when it comes to writing and drawing. Amazingly enough, though, they are often the most passionate about building—the natural remedy! The more they fine-tune their dexterity, the easier "school time" becomes for both of you!

3. Patience

Do you know anyone who couldn't stand to be a little more patient? Construction takes time. Slowing down, reading the directions, doing it over when a piece has been placed wrong or a sibling knocks over your creation... these are all valuable character-building experiences!

4. Problem Solving

Some children simply lack the ability to troubleshoot a situation and figure out the next step. Construction sets provide a structured opportunity to figure out what went wrong and fix it, if you're following the directions. If you are designing your own models, you'll have even more opportunities to problem solve!

5. Spatial Perception

Probably the clearest picture of how important it is to be able to mentally convert 2-D images into 3-D objects is that of a surgeon. Knowing where the spleen is on a 2-D textbook page isn't nearly the same thing as being able to reach into an incision and find the damaged spleen!

6. Creativity

Not every creative person has artistic ability. But construction can open the doors of creativity like no other tool. What if I move this gear over here? Could I build that bridge with only blue pieces?

7. Following Directions

Some children are natural rule followers and need to be encouraged to be creative. Others need to constrain themselves to follow directions, at least on occasion! If your child falls into that camp, construction kits are a natural way to encourage him in this skill, with the added benefit of a finished result he can show off!

8. Pre-Reading Skills

Did you know that a child who cannot duplicate a pattern will be a poor candidate for reading and writing? Not only that, but the use of pattern duplication is a proven approach to helping prepare children to understand abstract math concepts and higher-order thinking. But if you have a scholar who rolls his eyes at working with pattern blocks and sighs deeply when asked to replicate a design with traditional four-sided blocks, you need construction kits!

9. Grasp of Physics

Friction, force, mass, and energy are all basic physics concepts much more easily explained and grasped with a set of blocks and a ball than simply by studying a dry textbook definition!

10. Engineering Ability

Many "born engineers" are not drawn to textbooks. But set a construction kit in front of them and watch them explore pulleys, levers, wheels, and gears. They'll soon go from exploration to innovation, and you'll be amazed at their inventions!

WHAT IF THIS IS TOO HARD?

9 STEPS TO TAKE IF YOU'RE FEELING OVERWHELMED

Everyone has felt overwhelmed at some point in his or her education. Whether it's a groan from you as you pull a giant textbook out of the box or the despair from your child when he's read the directions five times and the robot STILL isn't operating as he wants it to, you will almost certainly hit a moment this year when you realize that an aspect of homeschooling is harder than you anticipated.

So, what do you do now?

1. Take a Breath
Just knowing that everyone faces this should help you relax a bit. This feeling will not last - you'll get through this!

2. Jump In!
Why are you stressed right now? Are you stressed because "it" is so intimidating that you haven't been quite ready to tackle it? If that's the case, the simplest solution is to jump in and get started. Could you read the first page together before lunch? What if you have your student find all of the pieces for step one today? Sometimes it's better to muddle through a lesson together than to wait until you're ready to teach it perfectly.

3. Step Back
Perhaps you're too close right now. If you're mid-project with incredible effort and totally frustrated by how it's going, try the opposite approach. Close the book for 30 minutes (set a timer!) and go grab lunch, hit the playground, or swap to a more hands-on project. When the timer rings, you and your student will be ready to try again with clearer heads.

4. Time This
Timers are an invaluable learning tool. If you're being distracted, try setting a 10- or 20-minute timer during which you'll do only ___. Or tell yourself you definitely need to tackle That Dreaded Subject, but only for 30 minutes a day, in two 15-minute chunks. When the timer rings, close the text and move to the next thing. Dividing your day into blocks of time can make a remarkable difference in your efficiency level.

5. Level Down
Did your student take the math pre-test before jumping in this year? Perhaps he is just in the wrong level! If moving to an easier level kind of freaks you out, it may help to remember that you and your student are not defined by his skill set in any field, and faking his way through by blood, sweat, and tears does not help his future self. Taking the time to back up and fill in the gaps, though, will benefit him forever!

6. Simplify
If you are trying to do every possible activity in every course, it's no wonder you're exhausted. By the time your student is in high school, he will need to complete 75% or more of the work in each course to get full credits. We're not advocates of doing the work in name only, but it's okay to watch some experiments online rather than completing each one in the

dining room. It's also appropriate to only do every other math problem in a section if your child is bored to tears with yet another page of addition. Doesn't that feel better?

7. Make Accommodations

What exactly is stressing your student (or you!) out right now? Is it the pen-to-paper writing component? Why not let him use the computer and type his work instead? Or perhaps he can dictate to you and you write for him. Make sure you're doing whatever you can to engage his best learning style. Encourage Mr. Auditory Learner to read aloud if necessary. Or break out all of the favorite fidgets and let Miss Kinesthetic work at a standing desk.

8. Get Help

Ask another teacher/parent to take some time working through the issue with you. You may be surprised by how much clarity you gain with a fresh set of eyes. (Our Facebook groups can be great for this!)

9. Get Professional Help

Check the publisher's website, the book's teacher page, or the kit's manual for contact information. Most of the

authors and manufacturers we work with are fantastic about helping and coaching those who get stuck. Not getting the help you need from them? Contact mail@Timberdoodle.com or call us at 800–478–0672 and we'll work with them to get that answer for you.

9 TIPS FOR HOMESCHOOLING GIFTED CHILDREN

1. Disdain Busywork

Your child wants to learn, so don't slow him down! If he has mastered multiplication, why are you still spending an hour a day reviewing it? Yes, he does need some review, but we've seen way too many families focus on completing every problem rather than mastering the material. One way to test this is to have him try doing only every other review problem and see how he does. If he can prove he's mastered it, he doesn't need to be spending quite as much time on it.

2. Go Deep

Allow breathing room in your schedule so you have time to investigate earth's gravitational pull or the advantages/disadvantages of hair sheep vs. wooly sheep. Remember that your child is asking to learn, so why pull him away from the subject that's fascinating him? After all, we all know that material we're interested in sticks with us so much better than things we learn only because we must.

3. Go Fast

If your child wants to take three science courses this year or race through two math levels, then why not let him? Homeschoolers can absolutely rock this because there are no peers holding them to a "traditional" pace!

4. Encourage Completion

Sometimes it seems there is a touch of ADD in every genius. Give your child as much flexibility as you possibly can, but also keep in mind that you'll be doing him a disservice if he never has to tackle something he doesn't feel like working on at the moment. Sometimes he may even be surprised to realize that the very subject he dreaded is the springboard for a whole new area of investigation!

5. Give Space & Opportunities

If you can keep mandatory studies to a minimum, you'll give your child more opportunities to accelerate his learning in the areas he's gifted at. Common sense, perhaps, but also

worth deliberately thinking through as you plan out your school year.

6. Work on Weak Areas Carefully

While you definitely want to work with him to help him overcome areas he's just not as strong in, you also want to be careful that a weakness in one area doesn't impede his progress in other ways. For instance, a child may struggle with writing simply because his brain works much faster than his hands. While we encourage such a family to work on handwriting skills, we also suggest that they try teaching their child to type and allow him to complete writing assignments on the computer. This lets him continue to build his writing skills instead of holding him back because of his lack of handwriting speed.

7. Emphasize Humility & Service

We have met way too many children who are obnoxiously convinced that they are geniuses and that everyone needs to be in awe of their abilities. Your child will be much healthier (and happier!) if he realizes these four things:

- His identity is NEVER found in his brainpower.

- Even as gifted as he is, there are still things that others do better than he does.

- He is much more than his brain. (Should he lose his "edge," he won't lose his worth!)

- His gifts are not for himself alone but for serving God and His people.

Of course, the goal is never to insult or degrade him, but to give him a framework from which he can truly thrive and be free to learn. With a proper perspective, he'll be able to enjoy learning without the burden of constantly assessing his genius and worrying what people will think of him. Don't weigh him down by constantly telling him how big his brain is, either. Encourage his learning, but don't forget to cultivate his character at all costs. In 10 years, his response to rebuke will be much more telling than his test score this year, so don't put an inordinate stress on intellectual pursuits.

8. Talk a LOT!

Talk about what he's interested in. Talk about the theories he came up with today. Talk about his daydreams. Talk about what he wants to study up on. Talk about why he may actually need to master that most-dreadful-of-subjects, whatever that may be to him... Not only will you be able to impart your years of wisdom to him, but you'll also know well the subjects he's interested in and be able to tie those in to his other studies, the places you're visiting next week, or that interesting article you read yesterday.

9. Relax!

Your child is a wonderful gift; don't feel that every moment must be spent maximizing his potential. As a side benefit, just relaxing about his genius may in fact increase it. Our own family found that some of our best test scores came after a year off of most formal schooling! Not what we would have planned, but a very valuable insight. Living life = learning, so maximize that!

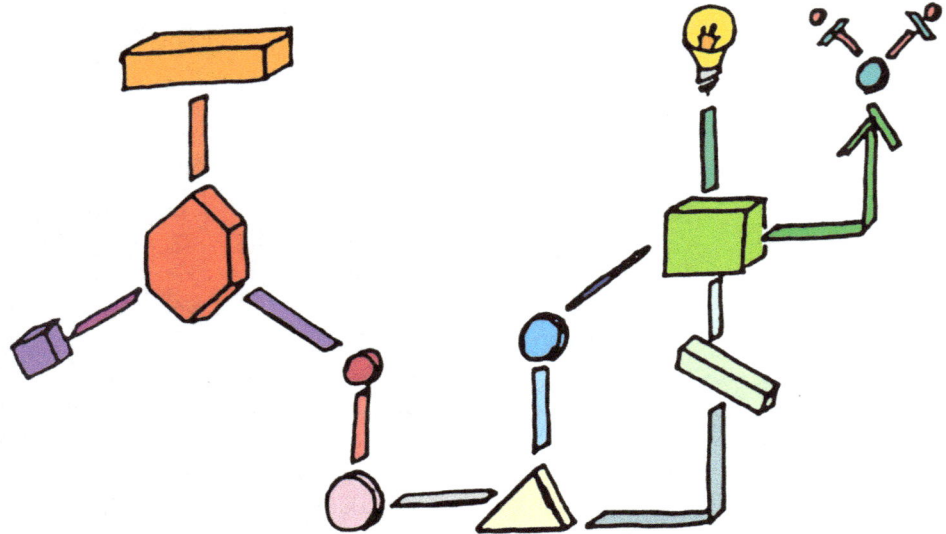

CONVERGENT & DIVERGENT THINKING

Have you considered the necessity of incorporating both convergent and divergent thinking into your learning time? Experts recognize these as the two major types of brain challenges we all encounter.

Does that just sound like a whole bunch of big words? No worries, let's break it down. Your child needs to be able to find the right answer when needed (math, medicine dosage) and also needs to be able to come up with a creative, unscripted answer when the situation warrants (art, architecture...).

A child who can only find the "right" answer will be a rigid thinker who can't problem-solve well or think outside the box.

A child who only thinks creatively will not be able to follow procedures or do anything that involves math.

What Is Convergent Thinking?
To go more in-depth, convergent thinking generally involves finding a single best answer and is important in the study of math and science. Convergent thinking is the backbone of the majority of curricula and is crucial for future engineers, doctors, and even parents. Much of daily life is a series of determining right and wrong answers, and standardized tests favor the convergent thinker. But when we pursue only convergent-rich curricula we miss the equally vital arena of divergent thinking.

Is Divergent Thinking Different?
Yes! Divergent thinking encourages your child's mind to explore many possible solutions, maybe even ideas that aren't necessarily apparent at first. It is in use when he discovers that there is more than one way to build a bridge with blocks, to animate a movie, or even simply to complete a doodle. Radically different from read-and-regurgitate

textbooks, divergent activities are not only intellectually stimulating, but kids love them, too.

Make a Conscious Effort to Include Both in Your Curriculum

Admittedly, because most textbooks and even puzzles are designed for convergent thinking, you will need to make a conscious effort to expose your children to multiple opportunities for divergent thinking. It is imperative because both divergent and convergent thinking are necessary for critical thinking to be effective.

Why Doctors Need Both Skills

As an example, let's look at a medical doctor. A physician needs to be extraordinarily skilled at convergent thinking to dose medications correctly, diagnose life-threatening emergencies, and follow safety procedures to avoid infection. However, the first person to wash his hands before surgery or to find a treatment for Ebola used divergent thinking. Some of the best doctors today are those who employ powerful convergent skills to accurately diagnose, paired with curiosity and divergent thinking to find the most effective or previously undiscovered treatment plans.

Convergent in First Grade

From reading to math, the backbone of your curriculum this year is convergent. This makes sense, because so much of learning at this level is simply marveling at facts. Sometimes there really is a right answer!

Is Divergent in First Grade?

These tools all include particularly strong divergent aspects to help your child become a well-rounded thinker:

Doodle Washington D.C.
Plus-Plus
Robotis
Imagidice

Plus-Plus and Robotis work both your child's convergent and divergent skills. As he recreates the exact models shown, he's working on convergent skills (and so much more!). But when he revises that model to solve a problem or builds a model from words only, that's capitalizing on divergent learning.

WHY ISN'T THERE A BIBLE COURSE?

OUR FAVORITE BIBLE TOOLS, 4 WAYS WE'VE DONE DEVOTIONS, AND MORE

From the time our children could sit in our laps, family devotion was a mainstay in our home, so teaching Bible to our children was paramount. But for too many families the sum total of Bible instruction for their children is Bible workbooks that are little more than read-and-regurgitate exercises, and that alarms me. Yes, we do want children to know the facts of the Bible – who killed a giant with a small stone, who was thrown into a lion's den, and who changed water into wine–and resources such as The Action Bible do a splendid job of teaching those facts. But my experience has been that children need massive amounts of intimate daily input to fully grasp the glory of the gospel, and there is no easier way than through a daily family devotion.

Then What About Requiring Children to Read Their Bibles Every Day?

That is certainly the trajectory we all want for our children, but how is that working for you personally? Have you ever had times where you 'read' your daily chapter(s) while thinking about dinner, the toddler meltdown, or updating your shopping list? Your children have the same struggles.

How Is a Daily Devotional Different?

With a daily devotional, the Bible reading can be explored in a much more personal manner. You know your child better than any publisher, and if the prescribed questions are not relevant to the sins and follies of your child, you can adapt and even drill down further. You can also use that time to point out how the Word is living and active in your own life with personal anecdotes that pertain to the topic at hand.

Then Can't You Include Devotional Materials with Each Grade Level?

No, for the simple reason that many of our favorite devotional materials, in particular Long Story Short and Old Story New, are usable for multiple ages and multiple years. And because God's work in each family is unique, we are much more comfortable exposing you to what we consider the best all-around resources and letting you cherry pick the most appropriate for your use and your situation.

What Does the Ideal Devotional Look Like?

We are ardent proponents of reading the Bible every day. For the little ones there is The Big Picture Story Bible, slightly older ones will enjoy The Jesus Storybook Bible, and then they should be ready for Long Story Short and Old Story New. But don't stop there; add in great theological books that you have enjoyed. When our children were little we read books by John Piper, Ravi Zacharias, R.C. Sproul, Randy Alcorn, and Martyn Lloyd-Jones. We read them slowly, sometimes just a page or two a day, pausing often to discuss the concepts and how they related to our lives, the lives of their friends, and the world at large. Every devotional time ended with a chapter out of a true-to-life story, both Christian and secular, where opportunities again presented themselves to discuss motivations, temptations, and how God's Word pertains to this situation.

Do You Have Specific Recommendations for First Grade?

We are big fans of:
Everything a Child Should Know About God
The Beginner's Gospel Story Bible

The Jesus Storybook Bible
The Biggest Story
Long Story Short
Old Story New
Thoughts to Make Your Heart Sing
Cat & Dog Theology...

And those are just the highlights! To see our most current favorites just pop by the website. (Also, keep in mind that if you have reward points on file, this could be a wonderful way to use them.)

What Do Your Family Devotions Really Look Like?

As you can imagine, this shifts dramatically over time. Let me give you four different snapshots from recent years:

2016: Herding Cats

As a foster family with little ones 1–4 years old, devotion time has radically changed from previous years when we were a family of grown-ups!

Our morning devotion routine starts with gathering the family and getting the little ones seated quietly on the couch. Honestly, this is probably the most difficult part! Some mornings are (finally!) almost effortless, but some mornings way more time is spent on obedience than on devotions. Not to worry, this is both normal and extraordinarily valuable for the children. In fact, the toddlers probably benefit more from that training than from the actual contents of devotion time.

Once everyone is seated, we briefly review yesterday's lesson and read a new page from Everything a Child Should Know About God. We're loving this book for our current little ones as it covers the basics in a paragraph or two every day–perfect for tiny attention spans!

We then do our memory verse of the week. Right now we're using Foundation Fighter Verses to help us select meaningful texts, and we're setting every verse to ASL sign. We're all learning and signing it together, keeping everyone engaged.

Finally, we end with a simple song, again with sign language. On occasion we've found a YouTube video showing other kids singing and signing, and that's always a bonus. But we've found that just learning it together works well also, and that gives us a much broader selection of songs to pick from.

All told, this is probably a 5- to 10-minute process. While more could be added (I'm eager to add more catechism components as one of our kids loves those), we're very excited to see our little ones learning the story line and theology of the Bible in a way that they enjoy.

In the evening we watch another chapter from The Jesus Storybook Bible DVDs together just before tucking our little ones in for the night. Much of it goes over their heads, but it is a wonderful way to end the day for all of us.

2017: Including Aspects from Church

Our little ones are now ages 2.5 to almost 5, and our morning devotions have shifted slightly.

Our main lesson now comes from The Beginner's Gospel Story Bible. It is as vibrant and interesting as our little ones are, and it does a wonderful job of presenting the gospel as seen throughout the Bible.

Our church uses The Gospel Project, so we end our morning devotions with this week's Big Picture Q & A, memory verse, and song. The familiarity of hearing the exact same thing at church on Sunday is really good for our children, and it's good for us, too!

This is still probably a 5- to 10-minute process. While more could be added, we're very excited to see

our little ones learning the storyline and theology of the Bible in a way that they enjoy.

We've already switched our evening devotions to an advent theme since we have high ambitions for their Christmas memory work. Each child is invited to hold a (battery operated!) candle and clutch a stuffed goat (from "the shepherd's flock") while we all sing a handful of Christmas carols and then recite the Christmas story from Luke 2. It is a wonderful way to end the day for all of us!

2018: Advent

We're forgoing a formal morning routine now, and instead whoever is working with the kids on any particular morning gets some Bible time in with them, in whatever format works best for them (rereading a Bible book, modifying a Sunday school curriculum, etc...)

Our oldest is also doing Bible time during her daily school time with Aunt Pearl, who has a routine adapted from Exploring the Bible where she reads portions of the Scripture as the five-year-old does her STEM work or other hands-only work. They then highlight what they've read to mark their progress. This child struggles with auditory processing so Pearl is always working to fine-tune the method and make it work for her.

At night, though, we all gather and light the Advent candles. (We chose the Advent Wreath with a new candle every day.) We then sing an increasing number of Christmas carols, adding a new one every week, and we recite a chunk of Luke 2 together. We end with a small chocolate for all participants.

This is a change of pace from our regular routine, and it

allows us all to absorb more of the wonders of the season together.

2020: Gratitude and Chaos

Our five little ones now range from babies to a five-year-old, and we're finding that we need to be punctual in our routine or the chaos ensues quickly.

The morning and school routines remain unchanged for now, and evening is when the formal Bible time happens.

After everyone is in his or her jammies and ready for bed, we sing a hymn of the week together. No one is reading yet, so we choose hymns with repetition and themes that will be relevant. (We're by no means a hymns-only family, but there is a richness in hymns that we so want our little ones to taste.)

We then read a chapter from The Beginner's Gospel Story Bible together, usually while the reader and the little ones sprawl all over the floor. We've done this book before, but it's been long enough that the kids are enjoying the repetition and getting more out of it this time through.

Once that is done, the "big kids" (ages 3–5) grab their gratitude journals and adult buddies, and together we write and draw something they are grateful for about the day. (The child dictates, we scribe and illustrate.) This is a concept we're still working to cement in their minds, but it is so valuable to both help their brains retain memories and to help them see every good gift as coming from God.

The kids reconvene in the living room a few minutes later for a chapter from a just-for-fun bedtime story.

So What's Your Plan?

This year has the potential for rich and vibrant growth in your child's life. Don't put off making any decisions or you'll end the year right where you started. We'd encourage you to jump in and try something. Not working well? Tweak it! Find the best time of day, content, and format for your family right now, and don't be afraid to make changes as needed.

HELP! MY BOOK SAYS "COMMON CORE"!

THE TRUTH ABOUT WHETHER YOUR TIMBERDOODLE CURRICULUM KIT IS ALIGNED WITH COMMON CORE

There's been a lot of buzz, discussion, and anxiety in the homeschool community for the last decade about the Common Core State Standards. Many of you have asked us what our stance is on the standards and whether our curriculum is designed to comply with them.

What Is the Common Core?

According to the CCSS website, "The Common Core State Standards Initiative is a state-led effort that established a single set of clear educational standards for kindergarten through 12th grade in English language arts and mathematics that states voluntarily adopt."

But Isn't That a Good Idea?

Growing up as an Air Force "brat," Deb, Timberdoodle's founder, attended many different schools throughout her educational career. She can tell you just how much easier it would have been for her if all of the schools covered the same materials in the same order. Then, she could transfer effortlessly between them instead of missing critical information because the new school had already covered something her old school hadn't addressed yet. So, yes, the concept may be brilliant, but there are some very valid concerns.

Why Homeschoolers Are Concerned

There is some real concern in the homeschooling community about what the Common Core Standards Initiative will mean to our families. In an early article posted by the Homeschool Legal Defense Association, HSLDA Director of Federal Relations William Estrada wrote, "The CCSS specifically do not apply to private or homeschools... However, HSLDA has serious concerns with the rush to adopt the CCSS. HSLDA has fought national education standards for the past two decades. Why? National standards lead to national curriculum and national tests, and subsequent pressure on homeschool students to be taught from the same curricula."

Declining Quality?
Some in the homeschooling community have also expressed concern that as curriculum publishers endeavor to align with the CCSS, the educational quality in those texts will actually decrease rather than improve, while some are disenchanted with the atypical teaching methods employed by the CCSS, among other concerns.

What We Are Doing
At Timberdoodle, our approach is simple. We are ignoring the CCSS and continuing to search out crazy-smart curricula, exactly what we've been doing for the past 30+ years. Our specialty has always been hand-picking the best products in every subject area and offering the families who trust us the same products we have used or would happily use ourselves. And we have no plans to change the way we carefully review every resource we sell.

Some Products Do Say Common Core
Some of the items in this kit do, in fact, align with the CCSS. This is not because we've sought that out, but because the quality resources we've chosen for our curriculum are already up to that standard or beyond. It is no surprise to us that the excellent tools we are excited about are also good enough to exceed the qualifications for the CCSS.

This Has Never Changed and Will Not Change Now
At Timberdoodle, we work with trusted publishers and products we review carefully, not just in math and language arts but in all subject areas, so that we feel confident we are providing some of the best resources available for your children. Every time an item we've loved is revised (or stamped Common Core), we make sure that it has not been watered down or made confusing. Our goal is to exceed educational requirements, not by aligning our curriculum with any government standard, but by continuing to find products that work well and meet the high standards we hold for our families and yours.

PLAYING IMAGIDICE
11 IDEAS TO GET YOU PLAYING

#1 Normal Playing
Have your child roll all the dice and then build a story that connects them all. For instance, "Once upon a time I was outside **flying my toy plane**, when I **stepped on a snake** hiding in the **vegetable** garden and I **was shocked**! Just then, a strange **smell** hit my nose. I followed it and found a **flower** I'd never seen before. I **jumped** up and down with my friend while we sang a **song** about flowers. Than it started to **rain** so we dashed over the **mountain** to get home to our **volcano**. The end."

We highly recommend starting with just three or so dice and adding more as your child's competency grows.

#2 Taking Turns
Roll the dice on the table. Select one that is face up and use that picture to start a story. "Once upon a time, a bad wolf ate all the candy. And then..." Now your child picks another face-up die and adds on to the tale. "He heard something that sounded like a storm coming. And then..." You're up next to add on to the story. Play goes back and forth until all dice have been used.

#3 Towering Tales
Have your child stack three to five dice to form a tower. Tell a story that starts with the top die and ends with the bottom one, working down the side of the tower and using every single cube in between. Now, choose another side of the tower and it's his turn to tell the tale!

#4 Feel These Stories
Choose an emotion of the day: silly, sad, happy, angry, etc.

Once your child has rolled all the dice, have him choose one for you which you use to tell a fitting story. For instance, the train could become a sad story: "Once upon a time I was trying to ride a train to get to Grandma's house on a mountain. However, the rain poured down, a volcano blew up, and we were left stranded on a stinky stretch of track!" Or a happy story: "One night we were running from a wolf when we heard a familiar sound, it was a train! We ran barefoot through the desert just in time to hop on the

train and ride cheerfully off into the sunset." Now you pick a die for him to tell a story about. Many of these dice have emotions depicted on them, making it easy to integrate emotional intelligence in every story.

#5 Tell the Story of...
Will you recount an epic adventure, building the story one die at a time to decide what happens next? Or describe your family's dream vacation with the rolled images of beautiful flowers, mazes, and hearts? Or imagine the worst — the shocked face, wolf, and storm icons make it easy. By determining the story line before you roll the dice, you're building a more advanced storytelling skill.

#6 Superhero Saga
Each person takes a turn to roll three dice and uses these to describe someone's superpower — either his own, or that of another family member or friend. (Also, choose a name — a name is very important.) Perhaps someone has the silent ninja skills of a snake, the drawing ability of an expert artist, or he is able to jump higher than anything.

Next, create a backstory by rolling all nine dice. Remember to add a flaw or weakness, as this is what makes your hero human.

Finally, all superhero teams need an archnemesis or super-villain to go up against. Roll all nine dice, then, as a group, choose a few images to describe this villain and give him/her/it a unique "calling card" or modus operandi. For example, The Sad Guy may attack by dropping tears on his foes, while The Mazer prefers to reroute his enemies' path. Give him/her/it a name and a reason for doing what he/she/it does.

Now that you have your characters, you are free to create all kinds of super-powered stories featuring the heroes and their archnemeses.

#7 Short Stories
Today split your dice into three sets of three cubes each. Now grab one set to be the beginning of the story, one set to be the scary middle, and one to be the happy ending.

#8 Start with a Book
Use the book you are currently reading to set the tone for where this story begins. For instance, if you're reading through Little House in the Big Woods, then choose Laura and Mary as your primary actors in today's story, set in the big woods.

#9 Keyword
Choose a word to use in every story today. This could be a vocabulary word, a new concept, or even a silly saying.

#10 The Set-up
Have your child roll the dice and arrange them, then you have to make up a story that makes sense of them all in the order he prepared for you. Now, having modeled that for him, you set up the dice and he tells the story as depicted!

#11 As Seen on Video
Today let your child take as long as he wants arranging the dice and practicing his story. When he's ready, film the story from start to finish and share it. He's going to love hearing positive feedback, and, in years to come, you're going to love having a record of this stage!

52 WAYS TO PLAY WITH MAD MATTR!

#1. Spoons & Forks
Use an assortment of silverware when playing with Mad Mattr this week. Can you make smooth paths with a spoon and curious holes with the forks? Which would you use to draw grass next to your road?

#2. Cookie Cutters
Roll your "cookie dough" out and use cookie cutters to make all sorts of "yummy cookies." Don't forget to sprinkle a little loose Mad Mattr on top of the finished product!

#3. Construction
Grab your smallest construction toys and use your bulldozers to push the "dirt" into piles or the backhoe to scoop it into dump trucks. Don't have any toys the right size? Spend your time making stacks of logs, piles of rocks, and other construction-themed resources. Our resident toddler loves playing with his trucks and has spent hours these past months digging, loading, and unloading.

#4. Cubes & Bricks
Using the table, can you make cubes with Mad Mattr? This takes a little practice, but it is very rewarding once mastered! Using your new cube skills, make bricks and build them into a wall. Too hard? Make a long "brick" and let your child use a knife to chop it into reasonable proportions.

#5. Pizza!
Squish about half of your Mad Mattr into a circle on the table. Roll much of what's left into a tube and slice it into "pepperoni" slices. Place them on the pizza, then sprinkle the rest of the Mad Mattr on top as cheese. Slice and serve!

#6. Archaeologist
Bury a toy animal or vehicle in Mad Mattr, then have your child use a spoon to "excavate" the archaeological find and reveal his treasure.

#7. Let It Snow!
This is a snow week. Can you make a snowman? A sled run? Reserve a little Mad Mattr to sprinkle over the finished scene–it's still snowing!

#8. Eggs
With Mad Mattr's unique texture, this is one activity that really works well only for it. Squish all of your Mad Mattr into egg shapes, making sure to press them firmly together. You want them to be very hard and compacted. Grab a sturdy bowl and "crack" the eggs on the side of it. Then gently

separate the two halves. (You can also break them apart by holding a half in each hand and separating.) Depending on your technique, you could get a clean break or, better yet, two halves with "liquid" Mad Mattr streaming down.

#9. Footprints
Go through your toy box and pull out any animals or dolls with interesting feet. Help them "walk" through Mad Mattr using firm pressure to get good impressions. What do you notice? Can you tell which animal left which tracks?

#10. Hamburgers & Sandwich Cookies
Use your favorite cookie cutter and slice three identical cookies. Stack them up to make sandwich cookies. Next, grab a circle-shaped cutter (or biscuit cutter or drinking glass) and cut at least three of those. They will become your hamburger and bun. Can you add a slice of cheese, tomato, lettuce, etc?

#11. Bag It
Use a clean paper bag or box for today's Mad Mattr. Make holes for your child to put his hands through and tape the top closed so he can't see inside. What can he make using only his hands and not his eyes? Make a few balls or cubes and put them in his bag. Can he tell which shape they are? How many does he have?

#12. Dinner Is Served
Shape Mad Mattr into a complete meal, and "serve" it on your child's regular dinner plate. Chicken and mashed potatoes will be easier to make than spaghetti and corn!

#13. Treasure Chest
Have your child find tiny toys and trinkets around the house, then encase them in Mad Mattr. Can he remember which item is where? (Mad Mattr is silicone-based, so stay away from other silicone items to avoid excessive sticking.) Or make small gems and coins out of tightly packed Mad Mattr and fill a small box-turned-treasure-chest.

#14. Money
If your child is past the choking hazard stage, raid your change bucket for coins. Use them to make imprints in Mad Mattr. Use the sides of the coins to make tracks, too!

#15. Snake Fossils
Find long objects around the house to use as your snakes. These could be dead headphone cables, charger cords for devices you no longer own, or even clean branches or vines. Create a stone slab with your Mad Mattr and arrange the "snake" of choice on the table. Then, press your stone over the snake firmly, creating a complete impression. Flip it over, remove the cord, and admire the imprint!

#16. Writing
Form your Mad Mattr into tablets, then use a pencil or stylus to inscribe letters or draw pictures.

#17. Beehive
You'll need a pencil and a couple of toothpicks or spaghetti noodles for this activity. Break the toothpicks/noodles in half for "bees"–you could even color them if you like. Now shape your Mad Mattr into tall beehives. Use your pencil to poke holes all the way through the Mad Mattr. Now your bees can go in and out of their hive!

#18. Make Bread
Knead the Mad Mattr and fold it into a loaf. While it "cooks" make a stick of pretend butter. Then slice the bread and top it with a slice of butter. Yum!

#19. Baked Potatoes
First, form potatoes out of Mad Mattr. Then, use a fork to poke them all over. While they are "baking," make a stick of pretend butter and slice it. When the potatoes are done, slice them, top them with butter, and serve!

#20. Hammer & Nails
Help your child draw windows, doors, walls, roofs, etc. on scraps of paper. Then, using a toy hammer and toothpicks, hammer the toothpicks through the paper and into a blob of Mad Mattr to make a house.

Variations:
Use a can or rock instead of a hammer.

Draw parts of a backhoe, ambulance, or garden instead of parts of a house.

#21. Scissors
Spread a piece of Mad Mattr as thin as possible while still keeping it thick enough to pick up (a bit thicker than cookie dough would probably work best). Have your child use his scissors to chop it up. You could even use a pencil to draw coupons into the Mad Mattr, then have him cut them out for you. (Or you could draw any other shape to cut out–the sky is the limit!)

#22. Apple Pie, Anyone?
Using a small bowl as a pie dish, press about a third of your Mad Mattr into it as a pie crust. Take about two-thirds of what is left and shape it into an apple or two, then let your child chop it up with a butter knife and fill the pie. Finally, form the remaining Mad Mattr into strips and lay them across your pie. Enjoy!

#23. Cookie Cutter Picture
Roll out your Mad Mattr, but instead of cutting it with a cookie cutter, just press it part way down, leaving an impression. What kind of scene can you make?

#24. Math
This week use Mad Mattr to answer as many questions as possible in your math book. Don't just talk about having five apples, then adding two more, but take the time to actually make them. This can breathe new life into math if the subject has become dull. It can also help clarify a new concept.

#25. Textures
Today is all about textures. Split your Mad Mattr into small sample swatches and smooth them each out. Then try pressing different items into your Mad Mattr, from

thumbprints to clean leaves or colanders. What's the most interesting imprint?

#26. Dessert Extravaganza
This week make every kind of dessert you can think of, from chocolate truffles to cupcakes to shortbread cookies.

#27. Gardener's Delight
Take about half of your Mad Mattr and create a garden plot. This could be as simple as an uneven patch of ground or as elaborate as a "raised bed" rectangle. Now use the rest of your Mad Mattr to make flowers or vegetable plants for your garden.

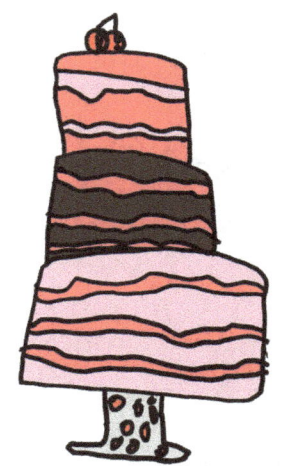

#28. Finish the Picture
Using an interesting page from any book you have on hand (coloring books work great), use Mad Mattr to make the image three-dimensional. Add dots to the butterfly, dirt to a dump truck, or smiles to faces. We've not had Mad Mattr stick to or bleed on paper, but that's no guarantee, so do use caution with what you're sticking it to.

#29. Cockpit
Take about half of your Mad Mattr and spread it out as a cockpit control panel. Use the rest of the Mad Mattr to make buttons, switches, and levers that "operate" your aircraft.

#30. Pretzels
Squish your Mad Mattr into long snakes, then shape each into a pretzel. How big is the largest pretzel you can make? How small is the tiniest?

#31. Paperclips & Googly Eyes
Using any paperclips and googly eyes you have around,

make as many creatures as you can this week. Paperclips can double as duck-bills, hair, or mouths–they also make great sculpting tools!

#32. Farm Detective
Collect a handful of animal toys with unique footprints and place them on the table. Squish or roll out most of your Mad Mattr until it is smooth and flat. (Flipping it over will make it perfectly impressionless if you're working on a smooth surface.) Use the rest of the Mad Mattr to make an egg, then break it in half. Have your child cover his eyes while you choose an animal to make tracks around and through the broken egg. Can he detect who accidentally stepped on the egg? Now let him challenge you!

#33. The Shell Game
Have your child use his Mad Mattr to make shells or cups. Let your child watch as you hide a coin or other trinket under one of them. Shuffle them and see if he can correctly guess which shell it is under. Or hide the trinket inside a Mad Mattr ball and shuffle it with a few identical ones. Can he find the treasure?

#34. Car Mountain
Use your Mad Mattr to make a mountain for your smallest toy cars. You could use a spoon to smooth out roads and even dig a tunnel through the base of the mountain.

#35. Dog Treats
Use your Mad Mattr to make all kinds of pretend treats for your dog. Standard dog bones could be rolled out and cut with a cookie cutter. Rawhide look-alikes could be twisted together. Small treats could even be sliced off a roll. Not a dog lover? Try making horse treats, giraffe snacks, etc.

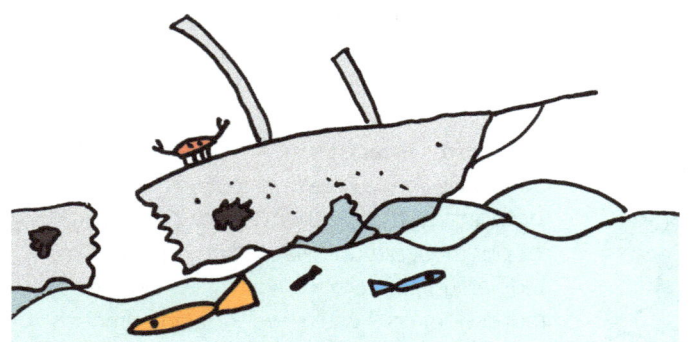

#36. Magnetic Rescue at Sea

Make a tiny boat out of paper and tape and fill it with paperclip "people." Use your Mad Mattr to make a tempestuous sea, complete with huge crashing waves. Place your figures to be rescued strategically across the scene, and don't forget to upend the boat or fill it with "water." Next, outfit your lifeboat or rescue helicopter with the strongest magnet you have and rescue all your stranded sailors. (If your magnet is strong enough, don't hesitate to plunge your people completely under the sea for a particularly dramatic rescue.)

#37. Treasure Hunt

Find some small fake gems or polished rocks to use as treasure (thrift store broken necklaces can be a great source of "jewels"). Bury the treasure in the Mad Mattr, then excavate it. Advanced kids may want to go so far as to make a Mad Mattr island and a treasure map, then carefully dig at "X marks the spot!" Construction-loving kids will probably want to use their toy excavators for digging.

#38. Castle

Use your extruders to build walls and pillars, then add moats, dragons, or whatever else catches your child's imagination.

#39. A Feast Fit for a King or for a Princess

All your food skills will come in handy this week as you "bake" cookies and make decorations for the king's (or princess's) birthday party. Do you have a child who would love to integrate art skills? Use scrap paper and toothpicks to make fancy flags or labels for the delicacies.

#40. Monster Trucks

Do you have any small monster truck vehicles? This week why not build a fantastic course for them to compete on. Include other cars to jump on, an airplane to jump over, and a number of hill-shaped jumps.

#41. Build a Zoo

Find all your favorite small zoo animals and then build each a spectacular habitat. Penguins love to slide, and hippos will be thrilled to find a large pond to swim in. Don't forget to feed all these hungry critters!

#42. Doll House

At our house making beds for favorite LEGO® DUPLO® characters is a big deal. Drape them with a soft Mad Mattr blanket, or make chairs and a table for the whole family. Mad Mattr can get stuck in small areas, so be prepared to have your child remove any lingering Mad Mattr with a toothpick if necessary. We've found that to be needed only rarely, though.

#43. Cupcakes

Get out your muffin tins for this one! After making the cupcakes, your child can decorate and slice them. You could even use scrap paper and toothpicks to make cake toppers, or utilize your child's favorite small toys.

#44. Pet Week

Does your child have a favorite pet or dream pet? Grab the

LEGO® DUPLO® tiger or PLAYMOBIL® unicorn and make a bed, special snack, perfect water dish, etc.

#45. Chop Chop!
Your eager knife user will love this week's project. Make hot dogs and slice them into toddler-friendly bites. Make grapes and quarter them. Chop carrots and potatoes for stew... We suggest using your child's real kitchen knives for this activity (only if properly supervised and if you have kid-safe ones, of course). It's great practice for managing them safely.

#46. History in the Making
What did you cover in history this week? Can your child replicate it out of Mad Mattr? The Silk Road may be more easily replicated than the marble palace of the Khan, but any attempt he makes will help cement the concept in his mind. Make sure to take pictures of his creation!

#47. A, B, C, D...
Use Mad Mattr ropes to create each letter of the alphabet in turn. (Don't try to do all the letters in one session!) Too easy for your student? Have him make something that starts with each letter.

#48. Nesting Birds
Birds' nests of various sizes may be filled with eggs and topped with handcrafted birds. More advanced creators may wish to roll Mad Mattr into "sticks" to use in constructing the nests.

#49. Bad Guys
You'll want a handful of superhero figurines, LEGO® DUPLO® people, or PLAYMOBIL® police officers for this one. Add in a "treasure" of some sort and now the battle is on. Can the good guys catch the bad guys before they escape with the treasure? What if you build a fort or hide the

treasure? What would happen if the bad guys change their ways and join the good guys? The storylines are endless!

#50. Dinosaur Romp
Grab your toy dinosaurs or make some out of Mad Mattr. Will you build a pleasant dinosaur diorama or does your child prefer the drama of dinosaurs turned loose on the town? Make sure to add some dino footprints and terrified (or thrilled) citizens!

#51. Your Child's Favorite Story
Does your child have a favorite book or story? You could build the bowl full of mush from Goodnight Moon or retell the parable of the lost sheep with a toy sheep and a Mad Mattr cliff. Add as many (or as few) props as you'd like, or recreate different aspects of the story throughout the week. (E.g. Monday: Papa Bear, Tuesday: Mama Bear, Wednesday: Baby Bear, Thursday: Goldilocks, and Friday: the bears' home.)

#52. Firefighters
If you have LEGO® DUPLO® or PLAYMOBIL® firefighters, this is the week to use those! Construct a building out of Mad Mattr, then help your crew rescue anyone stranded and put out the fire. If you like, add crowds of bystanders, ambulances for victims, and even handcrafted ladders or AirPads to catch anyone falling!

PLUS-PLUS

36 WEEKS OF CRAZY-SMART IDEAS

If you've read the previous articles, you're likely sold on the idea of implementing both convergent and divergent learning with your Plus-Plus set. To get you started, we've included one of each for all 36 weeks of a typical school year.

The model with a # has a picture for your child to follow. The goal is to make as exact a match as possible before he starts tweaking it.

The second idea has no picture or directions at all, so he is free to interpret it any way he likes.

Some models he will complete in minutes, while others will take much longer. If this is hard for your student, consider setting a timer for 15 minutes and asking him to work at it for that long and then move on for the day. You should also feel free to jump around and do the models that interest your child most each week. We've included checkboxes for that very purpose—you'll still know where you left off!

Week 1	Sword (model #1)	
	Your name	
Week 2	Cherry tree (model #2)	
	Something you'd wear to a special event	
Week 3	Apple (model #3)	
	Your favorite food	
Week 4	Butterfly (model #4)	
	A rocket	
Week 5	Teddy bear (model #5)	
	Something that floats	
Week 6	Watermelon (model #6)	
	A star or planet	

Week 7	Grandma's quilt (model #7)	
	Something from your neighborhood	
Week 8	Egg-sitting (model #8)	
	A bird or animal that lives nearby	
Week 9	Country road (model #9)	
	The critter you'd most like to bring home from the zoo	
Week 10	Traffic light (model #10)	
	Something ancient	
Week 11	Hot air balloon (model #11)	
	Recreate an item from your favorite book.	
Week 12	Old camera (model #12)	
	You're going on a trip. What will you pack?	
Week 13	Tulip (model #13)	
	Your favorite perk of being king	
Week 14	Snowman (model #14)	
	Something you like to do in each season (or pick one)	
Week 15	Pigtail girl (model #15)	
	The shape of your state or your state flag	
Week 16	USA flag (model #16)	
	This was in your science lesson this week.	
Week 17	Tiny rooster (model #17)	
	Your favorite mode of transportation	
Week 18	Ladybug (model #18)	
	A tool found on a farm	
Week 19	Man with baseball cap (model #19)	
	A person with an interesting job	
Week 20	Dragonfly (model #20)	
	A building or castle	
Week 21	Sunglasses (model #21)	
	Something from this week's history lesson	

Week 22	Penguin (model #22)
	You're very thankful for this!
Week 23	Royal crown (model #23)
	Something that is purple in real life (yours could be any color)
Week 24	Candle (model #24)
	A toy you played with this week
Week 25	Time for dinner (model #25)
	What are you saving your money for?
Week 26	Helicopter (model #26)
	Something invented after your grandparents were born
Week 27	Grandpa's coffee & cap (model #27)
	You can see this from your bedroom window
Week 28	Calico kitten (model #28)
	A tool you're not old enough to use yet
Week 29	Dalmatian puppy (model #29)
	A piece of furniture in your house
Week 30	Bird reaching (model #30)
	Something you'd like to give as a gift
Week 31	Giraffe (model #31)
	A fruit or vegetable
Week 32	Duckling (model #32)
	This is in your kitchen right now.
Week 33	Daddy duck (model #33)
	You use this to clean up
Week 34	Fastest jet in the world (model #34)
	Something scary
Week 35	Building a snowman (model #35)
	A baby uses this.
Week 36	Duck parade (model #36)
	This is the happiest thing in your house.

#3) APPLE   #4) BUTTERFLY

#6) WATERMELON

#7) GRANDMA'S QUILT

#9) COUNTRY ROAD

#10) TRAFFIC LIGHT

#11) HOT AIR BALLOON   #12) OLD CAMERA

#13) TULIP

#14) SNOWMAN

#15) PIGTAIL GIRL

#16) USA FLAG

#17) TINY ROOSTER

#19) MAN WITH BASEBALL CAP

#18) LADYBUG

#20) DRAGONFLY

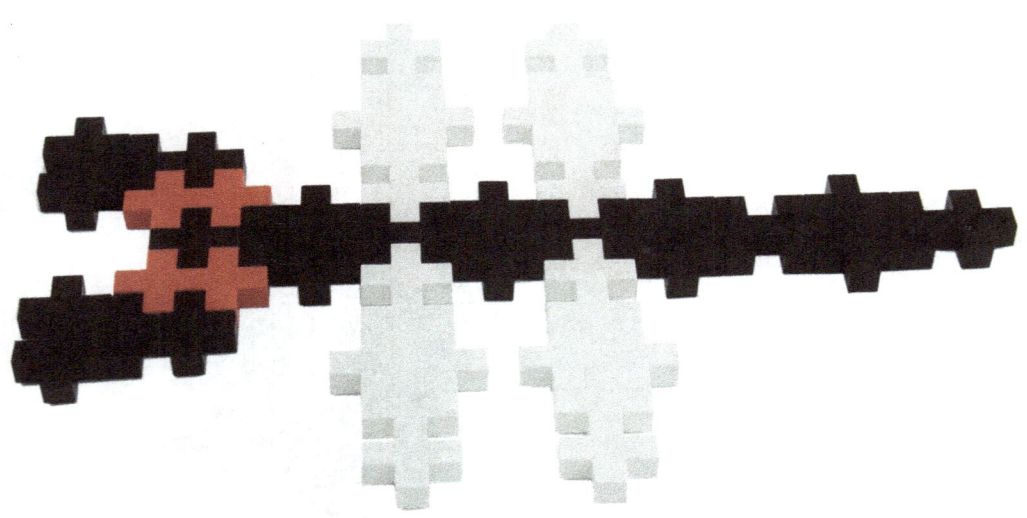

#21) SUNGLASSES

#22) PENGUIN

#23) ROYAL CROWN

#25) TIME FOR DINNER!

#26) HELICOPTER

#28) CALICO KITTEN

#29) DALMATIAN PUPPY

#30) BIRD REACHING   #31) GIRAFFE

#32) DUCKLING   #33) DADDY DUCK

#35) BUILDING A SNOWMAN

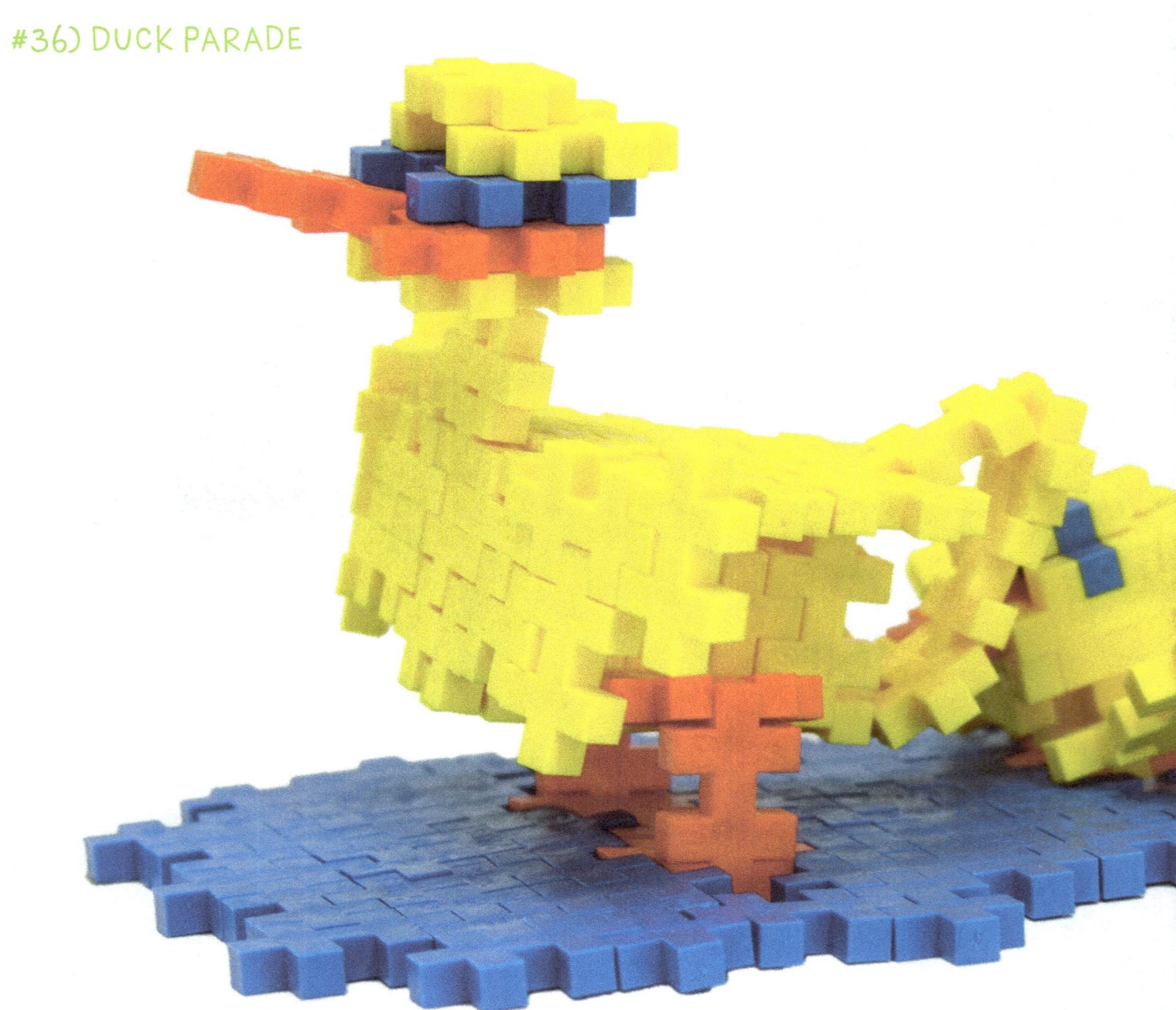

Thanks to David Kosor for submitting this USA map idea!

PLUS-PLUS 101

TIPS AND TRICKS FROM THE PROFESSIONALS

If you're looking for step-by-step directions to get your child started with more complex models, you've come to the right place!

Used with the permission of the publisher, these pages are where you'll see exactly how to connect various Plus-Plus configurations to make truly fabulous designs.

We suggest you work through these pages at your own pace as a supplement to the 36 weeks of designs, but feel free to tweak that plan to whatever best suits your child.

HERE ARE A FEW WAYS YOU CAN PUT 2 PIECES OF PLUS-PLUS TOGETHER:

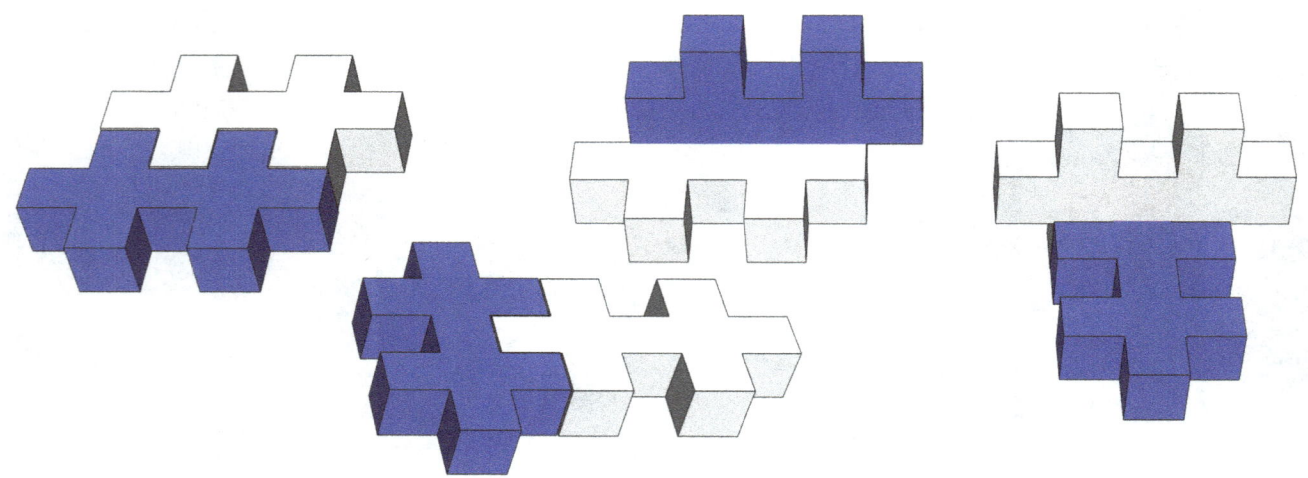

AND 3 PIECES OF PLUS-PLUS:

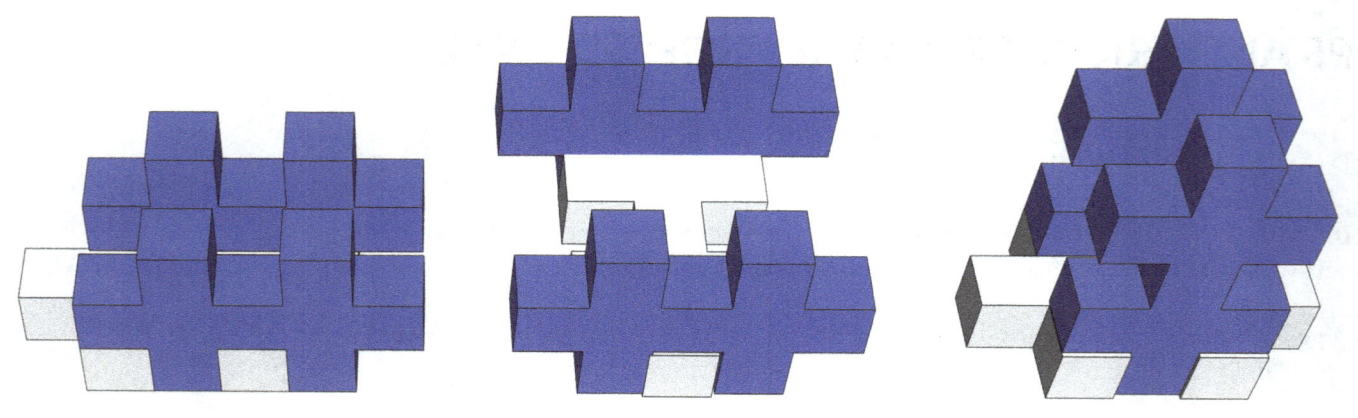

www.timberdoodle.com • ©2020

AND 4 PIECES...OR MORE!

YOU CAN BUILD FLAT MOSAICS WITH PLUS-PLUS – LETTERS, NUMBERS, PATTERNS AND MORE. TRY A FEW OF THESE!

NOW TRY BUILDING SOME FLAT PEOPLE...
AND THEN STAND THEM UP!

www.timberdoodle.com • ©2020

LET'S BUILD SOME 3D PEOPLE!

X2

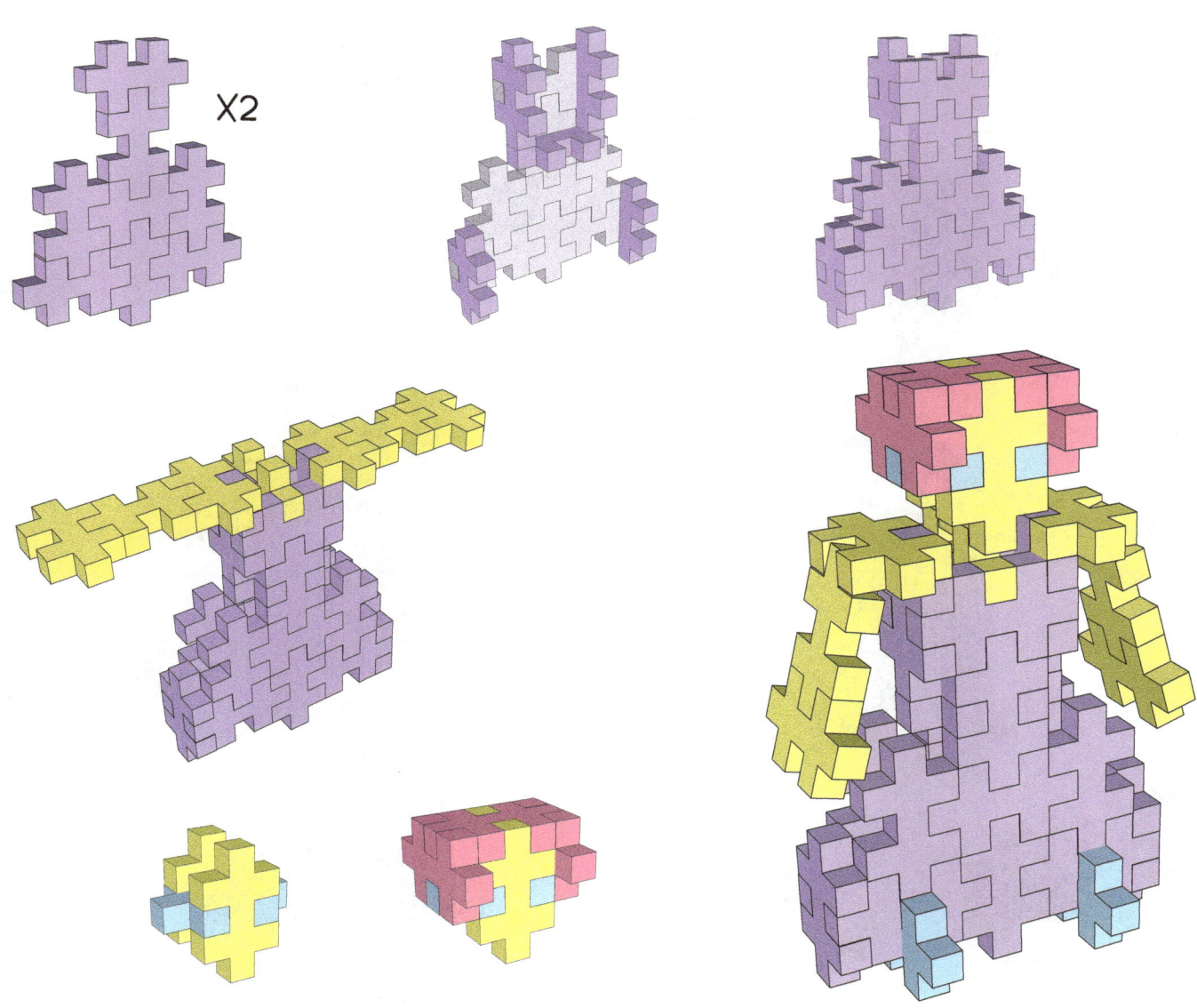

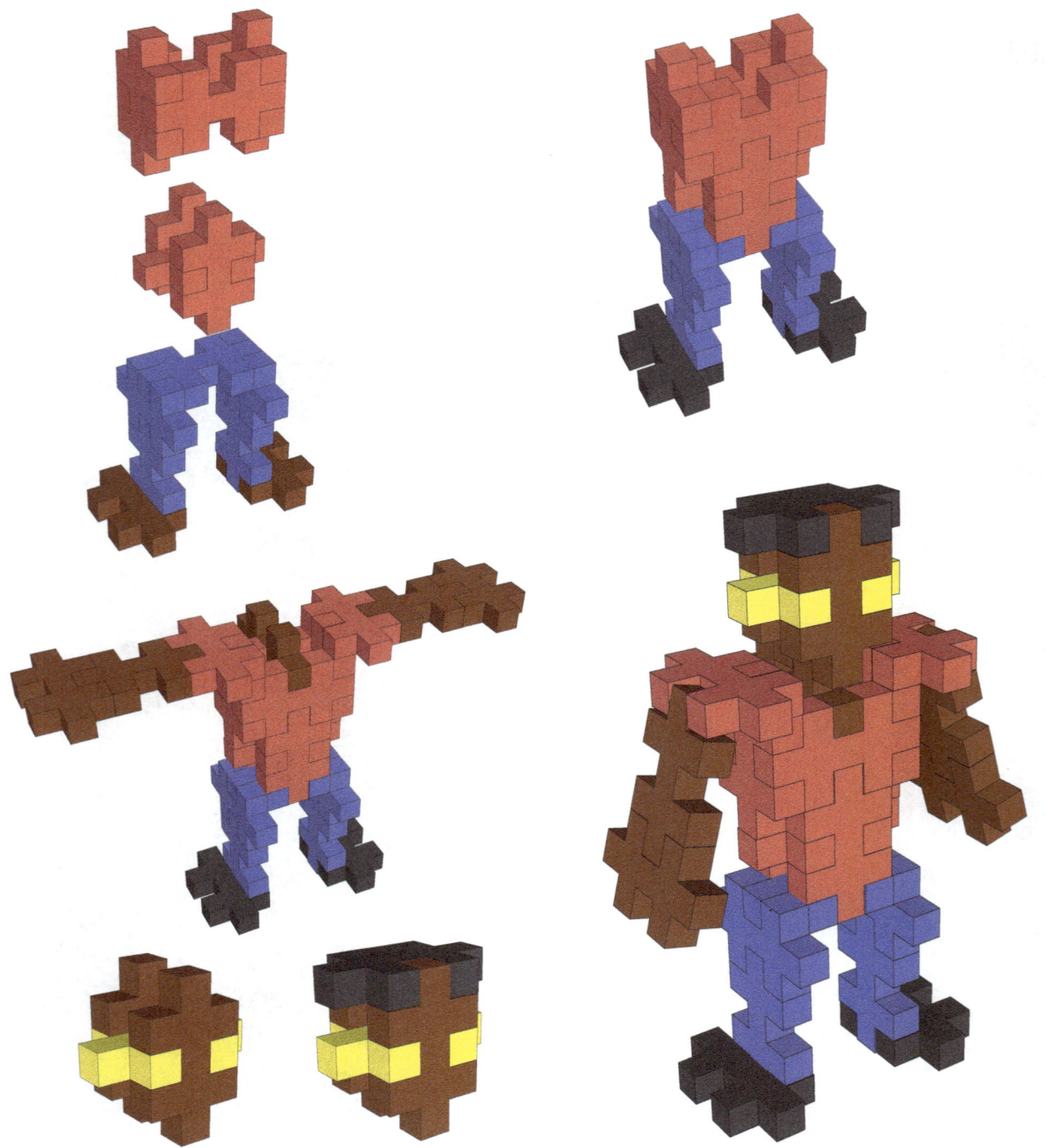

www.timberdoodle.com • ©2020

B U I L D   A   T O P

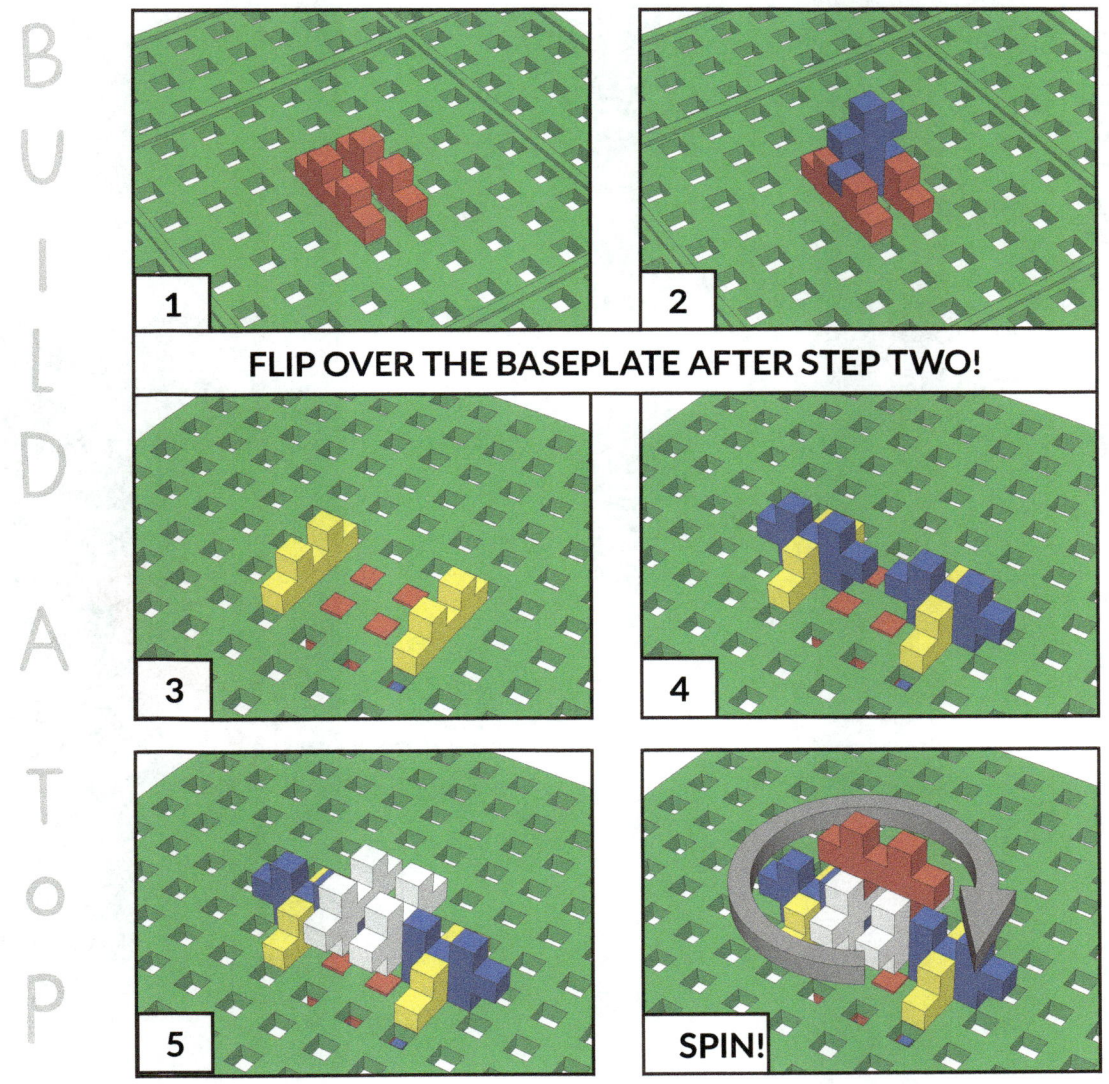

FLIP OVER THE BASEPLATE AFTER STEP TWO!

SPIN!

MAKE A CUSTOM MESSAGE!

BUILD SCENES

BUILD THESE FLAT MOSAIC PARTS AND THEN
MAKE THEM INTO A COOL 3D SCENE!

CASTLE

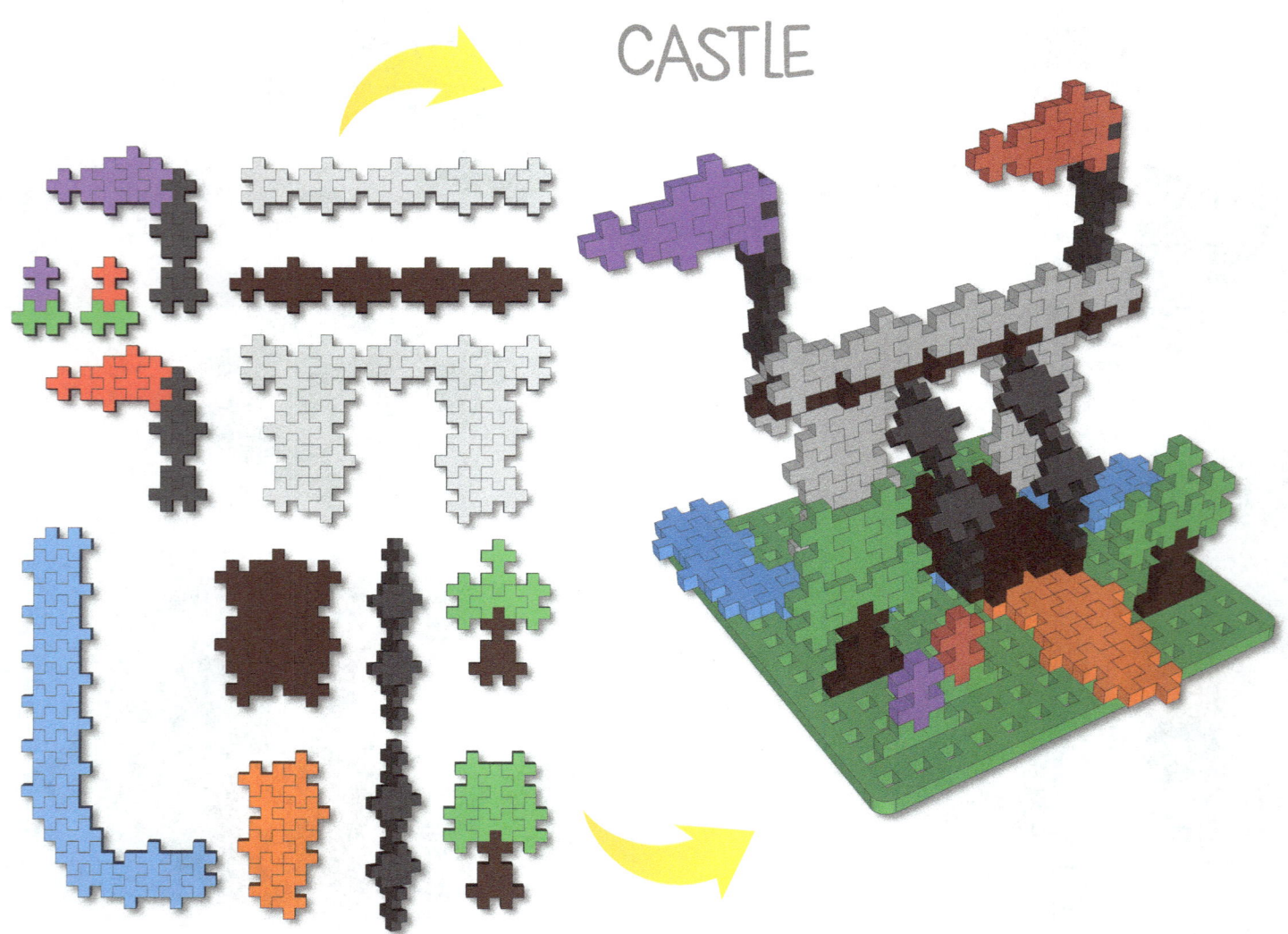

www.timberdoodle.com • ©2020

HOUSE

727 BOOK SUGGESTIONS

So you love the idea of the reading challenge, but you'd like a boost to get you started? You've come to the right place!

Customize This!

You'll find a few ideas here for each challenge, but don't forget that you're not bound to our list. There are literally hundreds more options that may be even better for your family. Use these pages as starter ideas and not as your final list.

Will I See the Same Books Over and Over?

No, not on this list! However, you can expect to see some of these books appear on the lists for more than one grade (so if you have a first-grader and a second-grader, some parts of the list will match), since books are often appropriate for more than one grade level.

Many books could easily fit into more than one category, but we only put each in one place on your list for your convenience. (Books that are part of a series are the one exception, as you may find an individual title in one spot and the whole series referenced elsewhere.) So if you're finding that you want to read more than one book from a particular challenge, the odds are good that skimming the list will give you another challenge to list it under. For instance, Where's the Big Bad Wolf? from challenge 33 (a funny book) would also fit really well under challenge 34 (a mystery or detective story), challenge 15 (a book of fairy tales or folk tales), or challenge 62 (a book about animals). Shuffle things as you like!

Repeated Authors
In this grade you'll find a lot of Biscuit, Amelia Bedelia, Berenstain Bears, Mr. Putter and Tabby, etc. Not a fan? Just skip them! But most kids love the repetition of finding the same heroes in a new story, so we have not hesitated to include much of the series throughout the challenges when appropriate.

A Variety of Reading Levels
Some of these books are clearly geared as a read-aloud at this age and would be challenging for most first-graders to read independently. However, most of the books do fall into the range of material typically suggested for a first-grader. Our suggestion would be not to worry much about which books are read by your student vs. yourself. Grab the titles that interest you and him, and then flip through them. Which is he ready to enjoy reading? Set those aside for him. The rest you'll read to him. As your year progresses and his skills increase, you'll likely find you are setting more and more books aside for him to read. Read-alouds meet your child's tremendous need for literacy, language, and stories, though, so never shy away from simply reading to him!

A Note About Our Book Ideas
If you've been reading to your child long (or if you've simply perused your local public library), you've probably noticed that families have very different standards for their reading

materials. The books you'll find listed here are ones that members of our team have read, have added to their "I want to read this" list, or have had recommended to them.

Even among our team there is a wide range in what titles our families would find acceptable. Some of us find fantasy objectionable and would skip books that obscure a solid Christian worldview but will gladly read a scarier adventure story than other families would be comfortable with. Others of us consider those fantasy titles to be an interesting addition and worthy of much discussion. We've opted to include titles with abandon, knowing that you will be able to flip through them at the library to determine if they are a good fit for your family.

So this is not a "Timberdoodle would sell these books if we could" list. We can't vouch for each of the titles, and we certainly can't know which ones are a good fit for your particular family. Mostly we're providing this list to give you some ideas, just in case you're drawing a blank in thinking of books for a particular topic. Use ideas as the jumping-off point for which they are intended, and, as always, we highly recommend previewing the books yourself.

Use Your Library
We can't overemphasize how useful your local library will be to you this year. We've listed multiple options under each challenge to try to ensure at least one title will be available. Now that most libraries allow you to place books on hold online, you'll find that you can use any spare hour in your day to request books for the next challenges. Then, whoever is in town next can swing by the library and pick them up. If you've not yet become a dedicated library user, this is the year!

Reading and Talking

If you're newer to reading together, our biggest tips for you are these. First, just read together. Whether you read a page or read a book you are making memories and building literacy. Don't overthink this—just squeeze it in as you can and watch reading time quickly become a highlight of your day.

Secondly, make sure you're discussing what you're reading. This doesn't need to be a formal book report on every book you encounter (please no!) or a tedious question and answer session every evening. Instead, talk as you go:

"Look at their faces! How do they feel? Why?"
"Do you like his choice? What would you do?"
"What do you think will happen next?"
"It looks like he thinks he is the most important. What's the truth?"
"What was your favorite part of this book?"

With these simple questions you are building emotional intelligence, worldview, logic, observational skills, and so much more.

Reading and Racism

It is worth noting that many of the books we grew up on have terrible racist undertones. (E.G. the neighbor in Little House on the Prairie who announces that "The only good Indian is a dead Indian," or those Tintin titles which portray people of color in negative ways.) We have kept some of these titles on our reading list because racism is a critical issue to discuss thoughtfully with your child, rather than just pretending it doesn't exist.

As our friend Tasha at Happy Homeschool Nest says:

What Can You Do: Teaching Your Family To Be Anti-Racist

Being anti-racist requires intentional and continuous action on your part as a mom. You set the tone for your home. Your children see what you truly value and believe. Waiting for "the right time" or when your child is "old enough" will be too late.

1.   **Point out racism in movies and literature.** Classics especially. Think Little House on the Prairie for a minute. Dr Seuss. To Kill a Mockingbird. Adventures of Huckleberry Finn. I am not saying don't have these books on your shelves, but I am saying read them with your child and discuss why the author depicted the People of Color in those negative or rude ways.

2.   **Discuss Hard Stuff.** You should always be explicit with children, of all ages, that racism is very hurtful and always wrong. Teach your child to be an ally. Teach them to speak up when they hear someone saying racist comments or jokes. Teach them to be a friend to the refugees, the low-income kids, the disabled kids, the Hispanic kids, etc etc.

3.   **Diversify your shelves.** Find books and movies about People of Color, preferably where the storyline isn't about diversity. Continuously expose your child to the beauty and richness of the world--the peoples, cultures, religions, buildings, fashions and foods. Watch the hard things. Read hard books. Don't shy away from the hard conversations.

4.   **Don't make racist jokes.** Period. Racist jokes are so hurtful because they are basically saying "you are so far beneath me, I can both conceal and express my prejudice and you can't do anything about it because it's socially acceptable —it's "only" a joke.

Looking for more on this subject? Her entire post on *How to Teach Anti-Racism and Why* is phenomenal. (We've quoted Tasha here with her permission.) Find her whole post here:

https://happyhomeschoolnest.com/blog/how-to-teach-anti-racism-and-why

Make This List Even Better

We love your book recommendations and feedback! Did you find a book you loved this year? We'd love to add your recommendations! Just shoot us a note at books@timberdoodle.com and let us know. Or were you perhaps disenchanted with one of our suggestions? Please let us know!

At the end of the year, fill out the Reader Awards on page 165 and submit that. We'll be thrilled to credit you 50 Doodle Dollar Reward points (worth $2.50 off your next order) as our thank you for taking the time to share.

1. A BOOK ABOUT BEING A CHRISTIAN OR ABOUT WHAT THE BIBLE TEACHES

Jesus and the Very Big Surprise by Randall Goodgame
The Ology: Ancient Truths Ever New by Marty Machowski
The Biggest Story by Kevin DeYoung
The Gospel Story Bible by Marty Machowski
Long Story Short by Marty Machowski
Old Story New by Marty Machowski
The Garden, the Curtain, and the Cross by Carl Laferton
God's Very Good Idea by Trillia Newbell
God's Great Love for You by Rick Warren
The Tiny Truths Illustrated Bible by Joanna Rivard and Tim Penner
The Berenstain Bears Storybook Bible by Jan & Mike Berenstain
Eric Says... series by Dai Hankey
God's Wisdom for Little Boys by Jim & Elizabeth George
God's Wisdom for Little Girls by Elizabeth George
Little Visits with God by Allan Hart Jahsmann and Martin P. Simon

2. A BOOK ABOUT THE WORLD

A Ticket Around the World by Natalia Diaz
Children Just Like Me by Anabel Kindersley
This Is the World by Miroslav Šašek
Little Kids First Big Book of the World by Elizabeth Carney
Usborne My Very First Our World Book
Stories from Around the World by Heather Amery
This Is How We Do It by Matt Lamothe
The Berenstain Bears Around the World by Mike Berenstain
Richard Scarry's Busy, Busy World by Richard Scarry

3. A BIOGRAPHY

Little Lights series by Catherine MacKenzie
Easy Reader Biographies from Scholastic
National Geographic Readers Bios
Step Into Reading Biographies
The Story of Ruby Bridges by Robert Coles
Abraham Lincoln by Ingri and Edgar Parin D'Aulaire

4. A CLASSIC NOVEL/STORY

Little House series by Laura Ingalls Wilder
Betsy-Tacy series by Maud Hart Lovelace
Make Way for Ducklings by Robert McCloskey
Mike Mulligan and His Steam Shovel by Virginia Lee Burton
Where the Wild Things Are by Maurice Sendak
Caps for Sale by Esphyr Slobodkina
The Velveteen Rabbit by Margery Williams
The Mitten by Jan Brett

5. A BOOK YOUR GRANDPARENT (OR OTHER RELATIVE) SAYS WAS HIS/HER FAVORITE AT YOUR AGE

Ask your grandparents or relatives. Or, if that's not possible, ask your Facebook friends for a recommendation for your child.

6. A BOOK FROM THE OLD TESTAMENT

This could be a literal book of the Old Testament, or it could be a book based on a section of the Old Testament.

Jesus and the Lions' Den by Alison Mitchell
Found: Psalm 23 by Sally Lloyd-Jones
Read-Aloud Bible Stories Volume 4 by Ella K. Lindvall
The Book of Jonah by Peter Spier
Daniel and the Lions by Katherine Sully
The Mystery of the Missing Spots by C.B. Martin
Jonah and the Whale by Erwin Grosche

7. A BOOK FROM THE NEW TESTAMENT

This could be a literal book of the New Testament, or it could be a book based on a section of the New Testament.

Loved (The Lord's Prayer) by Sally Lloyd-Jones
The Storm That Stopped by Alison Mitchell
The Friend Who Forgives by Dan DeWitt and Catalina Echeverri
The One O'Clock Miracle by Alison Mitchell and Catalina Echeverri
Read-Aloud Bible Stories Volume 1 by Ella K. Lindvall
Read-Aloud Bible Stories Volume 2 by Ella K. Lindvall
Read-Aloud Bible Stories Volume 5 by Ella K. Lindvall

8. A BOOK BASED ON A TRUE STORY

Herbert: The True Story of a Brave Sea Dog by Robyn Belton
The Bravest Dog Ever: The True Story of Balto by Natalie Standiford
The Whispering Town by Jennifer Elvgren
Lighthouse Dog to the Rescue by Angeli Perrow
Pocahontas: Princess of Faith and Courage by Maja Ledgerwood
Lucky Ducklings by Eva Moore
The Big Balloon Race by Eleanor Coerr

Clara and the Bookwagon by Nancy Smiler Levinson
Cora Frear by Susan E. Goodman
Fiona the Hippo by Richard Cowdrey
The Glorious Flight by Alice and Martin Provensen

9. A BOOK YOUR PASTOR OR SUNDAY SCHOOL TEACHER RECOMMENDS

Ask your pastor or Sunday School teacher. He or she will likely be thrilled to recommend a book to you.

10. A BOOK MORE THAN 100 YEARS OLD

Heidi by Johanna Spyri
The Wonderful Wizard of Oz by L. Frank Baum
The Wind in the Willows by Kenneth Grahame
The Tale of Peter Rabbit and Other Stories by Beatrix Potter
Raggedy Ann Stories by Johnny Gruelle

11. A BOOK ABOUT FAMILIES
Mouse Tales by Arnold Lobel
Amelia Bedelia's Family Album by Peggy Parish
I Love You Like Crazy Cakes by Rose A. Lewis
The Little Brute Family by Russell Hoban
Fancy Nancy: My Family History by Jane O'Connor
The Story of Holly and Ivy by Rumer Godden
Happy Little Family by Rebecca Caudill

12. A BOOK ABOUT RELATIONSHIPS OR FRIENDSHIP
Katie Woo and Friends by Fran Manushkin
Big Wolf and Little Wolf by Nadine Brun-Cosme
Waiting for Goliath by Antje Damm
Samson in the Snow by Philip C. Stead
Scaredy Squirrel Makes a Friend by Melanie Watt
Budgie & Boo by David McPhail
Fancy Nancy and the Mean Girl by Jane O'Connor
Frog and Toad Are Friends by Arnold Lobel

Cul-de-Sac Kids series by Beverly Lewis
Sidney and Norman by Phil Vischer
One Cool Friend by Toni Buzzeo
The Berenstain Bears and the Trouble with Friends by Stan and Jan Berenstain

13. A BOOK FEATURING SOMEONE OF A DIFFERENT ETHNICITY THAN YOU
Ziggy's Big Idea by Ilana Long
A Day's Work by Eve Bunting
Anna Wang series by Andrea Cheng
Dim Sum for Everyone! by Grace Lin
Grandfather's Journey by Allen Say
No Kimchi for Me! by Aram Kim
Whistle for Willie by Ezra Jack Keats
Looking for Bongo by Eric Velasquez
Shmulik Paints the Town by Lisa Rose
Flossie and the Fox by Patricia C. McKissack

14. A BOOK ABOUT SOMEONE WHO CAME FROM ANOTHER COUNTRY
Far From Home by Sarah Parker Rubio
Me and Mr. Mah by Andrea Spalding
Dreamers by Yuyi Morales
The Paper Kingdom by Helena Ku Rhee
The Map of Good Memories by Fran Nuño
Dario and the Whale by Cheryl Lawton Malone
All the Way to America by Dan Yaccarino
The Long Way to a New Land by Joan Sandin
The Long Way Westward by Joan Sandin
My Name Is Sangoel by Karen Williams
The Quiet Place by Sarah Stewart
Here I Am by Patti Kim
I'm New Here by Anne Sibley O'Brien
Emma's Poem by Linda Glaser

15. A BOOK OF FAIRY TALES OR FOLK TALES (OR AN EXTENDED RETELLING OF ONE)

The Princess and the Pig by Jonathan Emmett

Paul Bunyan by Steven Kellogg

Jack and the Beanstalk by Steven Kellogg

Chicken Little by Steven Kellogg

Hans Christian Andersen's Fairy Tales

The Tall Book of Nursery Tales

A First Book of Fairy Tales

It Could Always Be Worse by Margot Zemach

The Talking Eggs by Robert D. San Souci

16. A BOOK RECOMMENDED BY A PARENT OR SIBLING

Encourage your child to ask his parents or siblings for a book recommendation. Or, if he prefers to choose his own titles, have him ask for a couple of options from each and let him pick from that list.

17. A BOOK BY OR ABOUT A MISSIONARY

Lottie Moon: What Do You Need? and others by Catherine MacKenzie

Missionary Stories with the Millers by Mildred A. Martin

I Heard Good News Today by Cornelia Lehn

YWAM Heroes for Young Readers series

Granny Han's Breakfast by Sheila Groves

New Toes for Tia by Larry Dinkins

18. A CALDECOTT, NEWBERY, OR GEISEL AWARD WINNER

The Lion and the Mouse by Jerry Pinkney

Why Mosquitoes Buzz in People's Ears by Verna Aardema

A Ball for Daisy by Chris Raschka

My Friend Rabbit by Eric Rohmann

Joseph Had a Little Overcoat by Simms Taback

Zelda and Ivy: The Runaways by Laura McGee Kvasnosky

19. A BOOK ABOUT A HOLIDAY

Sshh... Don't Wake the Baby by Helen Buckley

If I Were in Charge of Christmas by Helen Buckley

This Is the Stable by Cynthia Cotten

God Gave Us Christmas by Lisa Tawn Bergren

Arthur's Christmas Cookies by Lillian Hoban

Christmas in the Big Woods by Laura Ingalls Wilder

The Berenstain Bears Give Thanks by Stan and Jan Berenstain

The Puppy Who Wanted a Boy by Jane Thayer

A Charlie Brown Christmas by Charles M. Schulz

Andi's Circle C Christmas by Susan K. Marlow

Sarah Gives Thanks by Mike Allegra

Cranberry Thanksgiving and others by Wende Devlin

The First Thanksgiving by Linda Hayward

The First Thanksgiving by Jean Craighead George

The Thanksgiving Story by Alice Dalgliesh

The Story of the Pilgrims by Katharine Ross

20. A BOOK ABOUT GRANDPARENTS

Drawn Together by Minh Lê
Between Us and Abuela by Mitali Perkins
Nora's Ark by Natalie Kinsey-Warnock
Dear Juno by Soyung Pak
In Plain Sight by Richard Jackson
The Hello, Goodbye Window by Norton Juster
Henry and Mudge and the Great Grandpas by Cynthia
    Rylant

21. A BOOK WITH VISUAL PUZZLES

Migloo's Day by William Bee
The Circus Ship by Chris Van Dusen
Where's Waldo? books
I Spy books
Usborne 1001 Things to Spot books
Disney Look and Find books
Highlights Hidden Pictures books
Seek and Find Bible Stories by Carl Anker Mortensen

22. A BOOK THAT HAS A FRUIT OF THE SPIRIT IN ITS TITLE

Somebody Loves You, Mr. Hatch by Eileen Spinelli
Princess Joy's Birthday Blessings by Jeanna Young and
    Jacqueline Johnson
Because I Love You by Max Lucado
The Berenstain Bears: Kindness Counts by Jan and Mike
    Berenstain
Little Critter: Just a Little Love by Mercer Mayer
The Berenstain Bears and the Joy of Giving by Jan and Mike
    Berenstain
Bob and Larry in the Case of the Missing Patience by Karen
    Poth
God Gave Us Love by Lisa Tawn Bergren

23. A BOOK ABOUT A FARM

Tiny on the Farm by Cari Meister
Farmer John's Tractor by Sally Sutton
Duck to the Rescue by John Himmelman
Winter on the Farm by Laura Ingalls Wilder
Trudy by Henry Cole
Farmer Duck by Martin Waddell
Old MacDonald Had a Truck by Steve Goetz
My Big Wimmelbook: On the Farm by Max Walther
The Berenstain Bears Down on the Farm by Stan and Jan
    Berenstain

24. A BOOK ABOUT ILLNESS OR MEDICINE

Katie Woo Has the Flu by Fran Manushkin
Patricia's Vision by Michelle Lord
Calling Doctor Amelia Bedelia by Herman Parish
A Sick Day for Amos McGee by Philip C. Stead
Mr. Putter & Tabby Catch the Cold by Cynthia Rylant
Brave Clara Barton by Frank Murphy
Itchy, Itchy Chicken Pox by Grace Maccarone
Florence Nightingale by Demi

25. A BOOK ABOUT SCHOOL, A TEACHER, OR LEARNING

Steamboat School by Deborah Hopkinson
The Oldest Student by Rita Lorraine Hubbard
More Than Anything Else by Marie Bradby
Teach Us, Amelia Bedelia by Peggy Parish
Andi's Scary School Days by Susan K. Marlow
Mr. Putter & Tabby Ring the Bell by Cynthia Rylant
This Is My Home, This Is My School by Jonathan Bean
Biscuit Goes to School by Alyssa Satin Capucilli
"B" Is for Betsy by Carolyn Haywood
Skippack School by Marguerite De Angeli

26. A GRAPHIC NOVEL

Toon Into Reading series
First Graphics: My Community series by Lori Mortensen and others
Pet Shop Private Eye series by Colleen Venable
Mr. Badger and Mrs. Fox series by Brigitte Luciani
Owly series by Andy Runton
Or check our website for other series we love!

27. A BOOK OF POETRY

Something Big Has Been Here by Jack Prelutsky
Where the Sidewalk Ends by Shel Silverstein
The 20th Century Children's Poetry Treasury selected by Jack Prelutsky
Poems and Prayers for the Very Young by Martha G. Alexander
A Child's Garden of Verses by Robert Louis Stevenson
The Llama Who Had No Pajama by Mary Ann Hoberman
The Oxford Illustrated Book of American Children's Poems
Julie Andrews' Collection of Poems, Songs, and Lullabies

28. A BOOK WITH A GREAT COVER

Let your child choose–it will be interesting to see what he considers to be a great cover!

29. A BOOK ABOUT FOOD

Ice Cream Soup by Ann Ingalls
Magic Ramen by Andrea Wang
Charlie the Ranch Dog: Where's the Bacon? by Ree Drummond
Fox and Crow Are Not Friends by Melissa Wiley
Seven Loaves of Bread by Ferida Wolff
Mr. Putter & Tabby Bake the Cake by Cynthia Rylant
The Seven Silly Eaters by Mary Ann Hoberman
Bread and Jam for Frances by Russell Hoban
The Berenstain Bears and Too Much Junk Food by Stan and Jan Berenstain
D.W. the Picky Eater by Marc Brown
Chicken Soup with Rice by Maurice Sendak

30. A BOOK ABOUT WEATHER
Under a Prairie Sky by Anne Laurel Carter
Terrible Storm by Carol Otis Hurst
The Rainstorm Brainstorm by Valerie Tripp
Henry and Mudge and the Wild Wind by Cynthia Rylant
Thunder Cake by Patricia Polacco
Mr. Putter & Tabby Hit the Slope by Cynthia Rylant
Ling and Ting: Together in All Weather by Grace Lin
I Spy Up in the Sky: The Clouds by Tamra Orr
Snowflake Bentley by Jacqueline Briggs Martin
Come On, Rain! by Karen Hesse
Storm in the Night by Mary Stolz

Oh Say Can You Say What's the Weather Today? by Tish Rabe
It Is the Wind by Ferida Wolff

31. A BOOK ABOUT AN ADVENTURE
Katie Woo: Every Day's an Adventure by Fran Manushkin
Utterly Otterly Day by Mary Casanova
Amelia Bedelia Goes Camping by Peggy Parish
Arthur's Camp-Out by Lillian Hoban
A Fly Went By by Mike McClintock
The Bears on Hemlock Mountain by Alice Dalgliesh
Otis and Will Discover the Deep by Barb Rosenstock

32. A BOOK BY OR ABOUT WILLIAM SHAKESPEARE
Bard of Avon by Diane Stanley
William Shakespeare and the Globe by Aliki
Mr. William Shakespeare's Plays by Marcia Williams
Usborne Illustrated Stories from Shakespeare
Will's Quill by Don Freeman

33. A FUNNY BOOK
Silly Milly by Wendy Cheyette Lewison
Little Penguin Gets the Hiccups by Tadgh Bentley
Old MacDonald Had a Dragon by Ken Baker
The Chicken Squad: The First Misadventure by Doreen Cronin
Who Needs a Bath? by Jeff Mack
Amelia Bedelia series by Peggy Parish
Parents in the Pigpen, Pigs in the Tub by Amy Ehrlich
Where's the Big Bad Wolf? by Eileen Christelow
Mercy Watson series by Kate DiCamillo
Tales from Deckawoo Drive series by Kate DiCamillo
Pigs Aplenty, Pigs Galore! by David McPhail

34. A MYSTERY OR DETECTIVE STORY
Who Did That? by Job, Joris & Marieke

The Missing Mitten Mystery by Steven Kellogg
The Chicken Squad series by Doreen Cronin
King & Kayla series by Dori Hillestad Butler
The Mystery of Mr. E by Valerie Tripp
Mercy Watson Fights Crime by Kate DiCamillo
Nate the Great series by Marjorie Weinman Sharmat
The Adventures of Benny and Watch series by Gertrude
    Chandler Warner and Daniel Mark Duffy
The Berenstain Bears and the Missing Honey by Stan and Jan
    Berenstain
J.J. Tully series by Doreen Cronin
Aunt Eater Loves a Mystery by Doug Cushman
The Zach and Zoe Mysteries series by Mike Lupica

35. AN EASY READER CLASSIC
The Cat in the Hat by Dr. Seuss
Go, Dog, Go! by P.D. Eastman
Little Bear series by Else Holmelund Minarik
Frog and Toad series and others by Arnold Lobel
Frances series by Russell Hoban
The Berenstain Bears Inside Outside Upside Down by Stan and
    Jan Berenstain

36. A BOOK BY OR ABOUT A FAMOUS AMERICAN
Johnny Appleseed by Steven Kellogg
The President's Stuck in the Bathtub by Susan Katz
The Secret Garden of George Washington Carver by Gene
    Barretta
Ben Franklin Thinks Big by Sheila Keenan
Harriet Tubman: Freedom Fighter by Nadia L. Hohn
Alexander Hamilton: A Plan for America by Sarah Albee
Martin Luther King Jr.: A Peaceful Leader by Sarah Albee
George Washington: The First President by Sarah Albee
Long, Tall Lincoln by Jennifer Dussling
John F. Kennedy the Brave by Sheila Keenan
Childhood of Famous Americans Ready-to-Read series

Abe Lincoln's Hat by Martha Brenner

37. A BOOK ABOUT ANCIENT HISTORY
Tut's Mummy Lost and Found by Judy Donnelly
Archaeologists Dig for Clues by Kate Duke
The Usborne Time Traveler
Cleopatra by Diane Stanley
The Usborne Book of World History

38. A BOOK ABOUT MEDIEVAL HISTORY
Saint George and the Dragon by Margaret Hodges
Joan of Arc by Diane Stanley
Marguerite Makes a Book by Bruce Robertson
The Knight and the Dragon by Tomie dePaola
The Hawk of the Castle by Danna Smith
The Knight at Dawn by Mary Pope Osborne
Castle Diary by Richard Platt
Knights by Philip Steele
Princess of the Reformation: Jeanne D'Albret by Rebekah Dan

39. A BOOK ABOUT MONEY
Does Money Grow on Trees? by Catherine MacKenzie
Arthur's Funny Money by Lillian Hoban
A Bargain for Frances by Russell Hoban
Little Critter: Just Saving My Money by Mercer Mayer
The Berenstain Bears Piggy Bank Blessings by Stan and Jan Berenstain with Mike Berenstain
Fox on the Job by James Marshall
Follow the Money by Loreen Leedy
One Cent, Two Cents, Old Cent, New Cent by Bonnie Worth
Alexander, Who Used to Be Rich Last Sunday by Judith Viorst

40. A BOOK ABOUT ART OR ARTISTS
A Dance Like Starlight by Kristy Dempsey
Katie series by James Mayhew
Famous Children series by Tony Hart
Getting to Know the World's Greatest Artists series by Mike Venezia
Come Look with Me series
Artists Books for Children series by Laurence Anholt
How Artists See series by Colleen Carroll
My Little Artist by Donna Green
The Chalk Box Kid by Clyde Robert Bulla
The Paint Brush Kid by Clyde Robert Bulla

41. A BOOK ABOUT MUSIC OR A MUSICIAN
Swing Sisters by Karen Deans
This Jazz Man by Karen Ehrhardt
Bats in the Band by Brian Lies
The Little Drummer Boy by Ezra Jack Keats
A Voice Named Aretha by Katheryn Russell-Brown
Sing to the Stars by Mary Brigid Barrett
A Band of Angels by Deborah Hopkinson
Mr. Putter & Tabby Toot the Horn by Cynthia Rylant

Mole Music by David McPhail
Max Found Two Sticks by Brian Pinkney
Francis Scott Key's Star-Spangled Banner by Monica Kulling
Charlie Parker Played Be Bop by Chris Raschka
It's My City! by April Pulley Sayre

42. A BOOK ABOUT AN INVENTION OR INVENTOR
Be a Maker by Katey Howes
Whoosh! by Chris Barton
A Weed Is a Flower by Aliki
Rosie Revere, Engineer by Andrea Beaty
Wendel and the Robots by Chris Riddell
The Most Magnificent Thing by Ashley Spires
How Things Are Made by Oldrich Ruzicka
Listen Up! Alexander Graham Bell's Talking Machine by Monica Kulling
Eat My Dust! Henry Ford's First Race by Monica Kulling
The Boo-Boos That Changed the World: A True Story About an Accidental Invention (Really!) by Barry Wittenstein
Balloons Over Broadway by Melissa Sweet
Oh, the Things They Invented! by Bonnie Worth

43. A BOOK ABOUT FEELINGS OR EMOTIONS
Freedom in Congo Square by Carole Boston Weatherford
Katie Blows Her Top by Fran Manushkin

My Happy Life by Rose Lagercrantz
The Rough Patch by Brian Lies
Dad and the Dinosaur by Gennifer Choldenko
Good News for Little Hearts series from New Growth Press
Something Might Happen by Helen Lester
The Clippity-Cloppity Carnival by Valerie Tripp
Listening to My Body by Gabi Garcia
Fool Moon Rising by Kristi and T. Lively Fluharty
All Kinds of Feelings by Sheri Safran
Jabari Jumps by Gaia Cornwall
A Whole Bunch of Feelings by Jennifer Moore-Mallinos
Feelings by Aliki

44. A BOOK ABOUT A BOY
Ready Freddy series by Abby Klein
Stuck by Oliver Jeffers
Yonie Wondernose by Marguerite de Angeli
Henry and Mudge series by Cynthia Rylant
Arthur series by Marc Brown
My Father's Dragon by Ruth Stiles Gannett
I Wish That I Had Duck Feet by Theo. LeSieg
A Big Ball of String by Marion Holland
A Fish Out of Water by Helen Palmer
Hi! Fly Guy by Tedd Arnold

45. A BOOK ABOUT A GIRL
Katie's Lucky Birthday by Fran Manushkin
Henner's Lydia by Marguerite de Angeli
A New Coat for Anna by Harriet Ziefert
Gooney Bird Greene series by Lois Lowry
Fancy Nancy series by Jane O'Connor
Little House in the Big Woods by Laura Ingalls Wilder
The Milly-Molly-Mandy Storybook by Joyce Lankester Brisley
Amazing Grace by Mary Hoffman
Cowgirl Kate and Cocoa series by Erica Silverman
Circle C Beginnings novels by Susan K. Marlow

46. A BOOK ABOUT BOOKS, LIBRARIES, OR LEARNING TO READ
Bats at the Library by Brian Lies
Amelia Bedelia, Bookworm by Herman Parish
Llama Llama Loves to Read by Anna Dewdney
Hello, Reading! by Martha Zschock
Biscuit Loves the Library by Alyssa Satin Capucilli
Least of All by Carol Purdy
Mr. George Baker by Amy Hest
Once Upon a Time by Niki Daly

47. A BOOK ABOUT ADOPTION
Star of the Week by Darlene Friedman
Through Moon and Stars and Night Skies by Ann Turner
I Don't Have Your Eyes by Carrie A. Kitze
Penny and Peter by Carolyn Haywood
Here's a Penny by Carolyn Haywood
The Mulberry Bird by Anne Braff Brodzinsky
Elliot by Julie Pearson
Wild About You! by Judy Sierra

48. A BOOK ABOUT SOMEONE WHO IS DIFFERENTLY ABLED

Rescue & Jessica by Jessica Kensky and Patrick Downes
Only You Can Be You by Nathan Clarkson and Sally Clarkson
Just Because by Rebecca Elliott
Susan Laughs by Jeanne Willis
Special People, Special Ways by Arlene Maguire
A Boy and a Jaguar by Alan Rabinowitz
My Brother Charlie by Holly Robinson Peete and Ryan Elizabeth Peete
Helen's Big World by Doreen Rappaport
Six Dots by Jen Bryant
The Girl Who Thought in Pictures by Julia Finley Mosca

49. A BOOK YOU OR YOUR FAMILY OWNS BUT YOU'VE NEVER READ

If you're a responsible person who has read every book in the house, feel free to use a book you've walked past at the library or a book your child has heard people talking about but has never read.

50. A BOOK ABOUT BABIES

Where's Baby? by Anne Hunter
JoJo and the Twins by Jane O'Connor
A Home for Virginia by Patricia St. John
A Baby Sister for Frances by Russell Hoban
Amelia Bedelia and the Baby by Peggy Parish
The Berenstain Bears' New Baby by Stan and Jan Berenstain
Biscuit and the Baby by Alyssa Satin Capucilli
The Year of the Baby by Andrea Cheng
Poppy's Babies by Jill Barklem
Babies Ruin Everything by Matthew Swanson
The New Small Person by Lauren Child

51. A BOOK ABOUT WRITING

Amelia Bedelia, Cub Reporter by Herman Parish
Arthur's Pen Pal by Lillian Hoban
Mr. Putter & Tabby Write the Book by Cynthia Rylant
Ralph Tells a Story by Abby Hanlon
The Best Story by Eileen Spinelli
Little Red Writing by Joan Holub

52. A BOOK MADE INTO A MOVIE

Charlotte's Web by E.B. White
Cloudy with a Chance of Meatballs by Judi Barrett
A Bear Called Paddington by Michael Bond

53. A BOOK ABOUT PRAYER

What Every Child Should Know About Prayer by Nancy Guthrie
The Berenstain Bears Say Their Prayers by Stan and Jan Berenstain with Mike Berenstain
What Happens When I Talk to God? by Stormie Omartian
What Is Prayer? by Valerie Carpenter
From Akebu to Zapotec by June Hathersmith

54. A BOOK RECOMMENDED BY A LIBRARIAN OR TEACHER

Ask your librarian, ballet teacher, karate instructor, Sunday School teacher...

55. AN ENCYCLOPEDIA, DICTIONARY, OR ALMANAC

This is unlikely to be a book you'll read cover-to-cover, yet it's definitely a resource you want your child to be familiar with. Consider reading a set number of pages or spending a specified amount of time and then checking it off the list.

The Usborne Children's Encyclopedia
Scholastic Children's Encyclopedia
DK Smithsonian Picturepedia
DK Merriam-Webster's Children's Dictionary

56. A BOOK ABOUT CONSTRUCTION

How a House Is Built by Gail Gibbons
Amelia Bedelia Under Construction by Herman Parish
The Ultimate Construction Site Book by Anne-Sophie Baumann
My Big Wimmelbook: At the Construction Site by Max Walther
If I Built a House by Chris Van Dusen

57. A BIOGRAPHY OF A WORLD LEADER

Nelson Mandela: From Prisoner to President by Suzy Capozzi
Martin's Big Words: The Life of Dr. Martin Luther King, Jr. by Doreen Rappaport
Malala's Magic Pencil by Malala Yousafzai
Peter the Great by Diane Stanley
To Dare Mighty Things: The Life of Theodore Roosevelt by Doreen Rappaport
The Church History ABCs by Stephen J. Nichols

58. A BOOK PUBLISHED THE SAME YEAR YOUR FIRST GRADER WAS BORN

You choose. Stumped? We found that searching for "best childrens' books of 20__" provided several lists to browse.

59. A BOOK WITH A ONE-WORD TITLE

Madeline by Ludwig Bemelmans
Tornado by Betsy Byars
Barkus by Patricia MacLachlan
Pond by Jim LaMarche
Begin by Philip Ulrich
Life by Cynthia Rylant
Storm by Sam Usher

60. A BOOK ABOUT SERVICE

Emergency Vehicles by Rod Green
Amelia Bedelia Helps Out by Peggy Parish
The Berenstain Bears' Neighbor in Need by Jan and Mike Berenstain
The Berenstain Bears Help the Homeless by Jan and Mike Berenstain
The Giving Tree by Shel Silverstein
Tea Cakes for Tosh by Kelly Starling Lyons

61. A BOOK ABOUT SIBLINGS

Little Brothers & Little Sisters by Monica Arnaldo
The Perfect Pet by Carol Chataway and Greg Holfeld
Dick and Jane books
Ling and Ting series by Grace Lin
Do Like Kyla by Angela Johnson
Tales of Amanda Pig by Jean Van Leeuwen
Louise Loves Art by Kelly Light
Best Friends for Frances by Russell Hoban

62. A BOOK ABOUT ANIMALS

Sparky! by Jenny Offill
Little Wolf's First Howling by Laura McGee Kvasnosky
The Animals' Christmas Carol by Helen Ward
James Herriot's Treasury for Children
Lulu series by Hilary McKay
Step Right Up by Donna Janell Bowman
Milo's Dog Says Moo! by Catalina Echeverri

Watch Out for Bears! by Ferida Wolff
Winnie-the-Pooh books by A. A. Milne
The Adventures of Adam Raccoon by Glen Keane

63. A BOOK FEATURING A DOG

Can I Be Your Dog? by Troy Cummings
Drop It, Rocket! by Tad Hills
Mucky Pup by Ken Brown
My Dog, Bob by Richard Torrey
Charlie the Ranch Dog by Ree Drummond
Ferry Tail by Katharine Kenah
Little Lucy by Ilene Cooper
Gaston by Kelly DiPucchio
If I Ran the Dog Show by Tish Rabe
Move Over, Rover! by Karen Beaumont

64. A BOOK FEATURING A CAT

Otis and the Kittens by Loren Long
The Christmas Day Kitten by James Herriot
Mac and Cheese by Sarah Weeks
Henry the Christmas Cat by Mary Calhoun
The Fire Cat by Esther Averill
The Last Little Cat by Meindert DeJong
What Cat Is That? by Tish Rabe
Niblet and Ralph by Zachariah Ohora
Dewey: There's a Cat in the Library! by Vicki Myron and Bret Witter
My Pet Human by Yasmine Surovec

65. A WORDLESS BOOK

Dog on a Digger by Kate Prendergast
Harold and the Purple Crayon by Crockett Johnson
Little Fox in the Forest by Stephanie Graegin
Wolf in the Snow by Matthew Cordell

Noah's Ark by Peter Spier
Ah-Choo by Mercer Mayer
A Boy, a Dog, and a Frog by Mercer Mayer

66. A BOOK ABOUT PLANTS OR GARDENING
The Tiny Seed by Eric Carle
Mercy Watson Thinks Like a Pig by Kate DiCamillo
The Gardener by Sarah Stewart
Oswald's Garden by Heather Feldman
Up in the Garden and Down in the Dirt by Kate Messner
A Seed is Sleepy by Dianna Aston
The Carrot Seed by Ruth Krauss
The Emperor's Garden by Ferida Wolff

67. A BOOK ABOUT A HOBBY OR A SKILL YOU WANT TO LEARN
You choose! Is there something that your child would enjoy learning? From science experiments to building a fort, there's a book for everything. Keep in mind that the skill doesn't have to be feasible to use right away. Choosing a horse or flying a space ship are fair game!

68. A BOOK OF COMICS
Peanuts by Charles Schulz

Family Circus by Bil Keane
Calvin and Hobbes by Bill Watterson
Red and Rover by Brian Basset

69. A BOOK ABOUT A FAMOUS WAR
Pink and Say by Patricia Polacco
Primrose Day by Carolyn Haywood
Welcome to Molly's World by Catherine Gourley
Revolutionary War on Wednesday by Mary Pope Osborne
Civil War on Sunday by Mary Pope Osborne

70. A BOOK ABOUT SPORTS
Jump! by Floyd Cooper
Bats at the Ballgame by Brian Lies
Play Ball, Amelia Bedelia by Peggy Parish
Mr. Putter & Tabby Drop the Ball by Cynthia Rylant
Pass the Ball, Mo! by David A. Adler
The Berenstain Bears Play Ball by Stan and Jan Berenstain
Betsy and the Boys by Carolyn Haywood
Brothers at Bat by Audrey Vernick
The Streak by Barb Rosenstock
T Is for Tutu: A Ballet Alphabet by Kurt Browning

71. A BOOK ABOUT MATH
God Counts by Irene Sun
Millions to Measure by David M. Schwartz
Ben Franklin and the Magic Squares by Frank Murphy
The Fly on the Ceiling by Julie Glass
Life of Fred series
Mystery Math by David A. Adler
Sir Cumference series by Cindy Neuschwander
The Lion's Share by Matthew McElligott
One Grain of Rice by Demi
6 Sticks by Molly Coxe

72. A BOOK ABOUT SUFFERING OR POVERTY

Pablo Finds a Treasure by Andrée Poulin
The Hundred Dresses by Eleanor Estes
Henry's Freedom Box by Ellen Levine
Esperanza Rising by Pam Muñoz Ryan
Dust for Dinner by Ann Turner
The Patchwork Bike by Maxine Beneba Clarke
I Am a Bear by Jean-Francois Dumont

73. A BOOK BY YOUR FAVORITE AUTHOR

Your child will choose this one, though you may have to help him think through his favorite books to narrow down the author he's enjoying most right now.

74. A BOOK YOU'VE READ BEFORE

Your child should choose, and make sure you mark it down since it's obviously one he finds interesting!

75. A BOOK WITH AN UGLY COVER

Let your child choose, of course, and make sure to document what he thinks is ugly about it!

76. A BOOK ABOUT SOMEONE ELSE'S FAVORITE SUBJECT

Does your child have a sibling who loves math or painting, a friend enthralled with laws or construction, or perhaps a grandparent who serves as a police officer or NICU nurse? Help him find a book about one of these subjects to enjoy, and maybe even to share with his friend or relative who inspired this selection!

77. A BOOK ABOUT TRAVEL OR TRANSPORTATION

Truckery Rhymes by Jon Scieszka
Monkey on the Run by Leo Timmers
Who Is Driving? by Leo Timmers
Mercy Watson Goes for a Ride by Kate DiCamillo
Let's Go for a Drive! by Mo Willems
LaRue Across America by Mark Teague
The Relatives Came by Cynthia Rylant
Fred and Ted's Road Trip by Peter Eastman
Arthur's Family Vacation by Marc Brown
On the Road by Lucy Nolan
Road Trip by Roger Eschbacher

78. A BOOK ABOUT THE NATURAL WORLD

Scaredy Squirrel Goes Camping by Melanie Watt
Crinkleroot's Guide series by Jim Arnosky
Willa's Wilderness Campout by Valerie Tripp
I Took a Walk by Henry Cole
On the Way to the Beach by Henry Cole
Little Critter: Exploring the Great Outdoors by Mercer Mayer
Take a Hike, Teddy Roosevelt! by Frank Murphy
Pony Scouts: The Camping Trip by Catherine Hapka
The Camping Trip That Changed America by Barb Rosenstock
A Pocketful of Cricket by Rebecca Caudill
Over and Under the Pond by Kate Messner
A Camping Spree with Mr. Magee by Chris Van Dusen

79. A BIOGRAPHY OF AN AUTHOR

Just Like Beverly by Vicki Conrad
Big Machines: The Story of Virginia Lee Burton by Sherri Duskey Rinker

A Boy, a Mouse, and a Spider--The Story of E. B. White by
  Barbara Herkert
John Ronald's Dragons: The Story of J. R. R. Tolkien by Caroline
  McAlister
A Poem for Peter by Andrea Davis Pinkney

80. A BOOK PUBLISHED IN 2020-2021
Your librarian should be able to point you towards the
new releases that are age-appropriate (you may want to
preview them, though!) or you can watch to see what's being
featured in your favorite book-seller's email or storefront.
Of course, you could also expand this category to be any
brand-new book or new-to-your-library title.

81. A HISTORICAL FICTION BOOK
All Different Now by Angela Johnson
Across the Wide Dark Sea by Jean Van Leeuwen
Clipper Ship by Thomas P. Lewis
Sam the Minuteman by Nathaniel Benchley
Prairie Friends by Nancy Smiler Levinson
Daniel's Duck by Clyde Robert Bulla

82. A BOOK ABOUT SCIENCE OR A SCIENTIST
The Magic School Bus books by Joanna Cole

Wells of Knowledge Science series
Mesmerized by Mara Rockliff
Indescribable by Louie Giglio
The Berenstain Bears' Big Book of Science and Nature by Stan
  and Jan Berenstain
DK Look I'm a Scientist

83. A BOOK ABOUT SAFETY OR SURVIVAL
Do your kids know both when and how to call 911? As
landlines become less common, you will want to make sure
that your child knows how to access 911 on the actual
devices he has access to every day. You won't see that
specifically addressed in these books, but it is worth setting
some time aside to discuss this with your child. (BTW, if
you accidentally actually dial 911 stay on the line. Every
department is different, but here our police department
is obligated to investigate every 911 hang-up for obvious
reasons. If you stay on the line and explain, that will save
everyone some time.)

This is also a great opportunity to visit your local fire and
police departments for a tour. Your child will learn a ton
about his community, and they often have helpful handouts—
for instance, fire escape planning info, etc.

Kids to the Rescue! by Maribeth Boelts
Who's Bad and Who's Good, Little Red Riding Hood? by Steve
  Smallman
Plan and Prepare! by Charles Ghigna
Officer Buckle and Gloria by Peggy Rathmann
Arthur's Fire Drill by Marc Brown
The Berenstain Bears Learn About Strangers by Stan and Jan
  Berenstain

84. A BOOK ABOUT SPACE OR AN ASTRONAUT

The Moon Over Star by Dianna Hutts Aston
LEGO City: 3, 2, 1 Liftoff! by Scholastic
The Ultimate Book of Space by Anne-Sophie Baumann
Mr. Putter & Tabby See the Stars by Cynthia Rylant
Moonwalk: The First Trip to the Moon by Judy Donnelly
Mae Among the Stars by Roda Ahmed
A Kite for Moon by Jane Yolen
Caroline's Comets by Emily Arnold McCully
The Magic School Bus Lost in the Solar System by Joanna Cole

85. A BOOK SET IN CENTRAL OR SOUTH AMERICA

Hill of Fire by Thomas P. Lewis
A Bear for Miguel by Elaine Marie Alphin
Ada's Violin by Susan Hood
Love and Roast Chicken by Barbara Knutson
Waiting for the Biblioburro by Monica Brown
Ready to Read: Living in Brazil | Mexico

86. A BOOK SET IN AFRICA

The Water Princess by Susan Verde
Yuvi's Candy Tree by Lesley Simpson
Anna & Samia by Paul Meisel
Jamela's Dress by Niki Daly
Anna Hibiscus series by Atinuke
Akissi by Marguerite Abouet
Mama Miti by Donna Jo Napoli
Mufaro's Beautiful Daughters by John Steptoe
Ready to Read: Living in South Africa

87. A BOOK SET IN ASIA

Little One-Inch and Other Japanese Children's Favorite Stories
    compiled by Florence Sakade
Ruby's Wish by Shirin Yim Bridges
Manjhi Moves a Mountain by Nancy Churnin
The Whispering Cloth by Pegi Deitz Shea
The Story About Ping by Marjorie Flack
The Trip Back Home by Janet S. Wong
Tikki Tikki Tembo by Arlene Mosel
A Grain of Rice by Helena Clare Pittman
Ready to Read: Living in China | India | South Korea

88. A BOOK SET IN EUROPE

Madeline series by Ludwig Bemelmans
Ready to Read: Living in Italy

A Walk in London by Salvatore Rubbino
The Story of Ferdinand by Munro Leaf
The Hat by Jan Brett

How Do Dinosaurs Eat Their Food? by Jane Yolen
Mind Your Manners, B.B. Wolf by Judy Sierra

91. A BOOK ABOUT SPRING
Albert's Tree by Jenni Desmond
And Then It's Spring by Julie Fogliano
The Riddle of the Robin by Valerie Tripp
Frog and Toad All Year by Arnold Lobel
Fletcher and the Springtime Blossoms by Julia Rawlinson
Spring Story by Jill Barklem
When Spring Comes by Kevin Henkes
Spring Surprises by Anna Jane Hays

92. A BOOK ABOUT SUMMER
Willa's Butterfly Ballet by Judy Katschke
Andi's Indian Summer by Susan K. Marlow
Ice Cream Summer by Peter Sis
Summer Story by Jill Barklem
Fireflies by Julie Brinckloe
Amanda Pig and the Really Hot Day by Jean Van Leeuwen
The Night Before Summer Vacation by Natasha Wing

89. A BOOK WITH A COLOR IN ITS TITLE
Go to Bed, Blue by Bonnie Bader
Red Sky at Night by Elly MacKay
Jonathan and the Big Blue Boat by Philip C. Stead
The Case of the Weird Blue Chicken by Doreen Cronin
Green Eggs and Ham by Dr. Seuss
A Splash of Red by Jen Bryant
Big Red Lollipop by Rukhsana Khan
Blue on Blue by Dianne White

90. A BOOK ABOUT MANNERS
Share, Big Bear, Share! by Maureen Wright
Dear Mr. Washington by Lynn Cullen
Richard Scarry's Please and Thank You Book by Richard Scarry
Richard Scarry's Polite Elephant by Richard Scarry
What If Everybody Did That? by Ellen Javernick
Do Unto Otters by Laurie Keller

93. A BOOK ABOUT AUTUMN
Bear Has a Story to Tell by Philip C. Stead
Ashlyn's Fall Fiesta by Meredith Rusu
The Muddily-Puddily Show by Valerie Tripp
Now It's Fall by Lois Lenski
Autumn Story by Jill Barklem
Flora's Very Windy Day by Jeanne Birdsall
County Fair by Laura Ingalls Wilder
Four Friends in Autumn by Tomie dePaola
Pumpkin Soup by Helen Cooper

94. A BOOK ABOUT WINTER
Utterly Otterly Night by Mary Casanova
The Storm Whale in Winter by Benji Davies
Waiting for Winter by Sebastian Meschenmoser
Big Snow by Jonathan Bean
Snowshoe Thompson by Nancy Smiler Levinson
The Snowy Day by Ezra Jack Keats
Winter Story by Jill Barklem
Extra Yarn by Mac Barnett
Mice Skating by Annie Silvestro

95. A BOOK ABOUT HOME
Vincent Comes Home by Jessixa Bagley and Aaron Bagley
The Berenstain Bears and the Messy Room by Stan Berenstain and Jan Berenstain
Over and Under the Snow by Kate Messner
This Is the House That Was Tidy & Neat by Teri Sloat
If You Lived Here: Houses of the World by Giles Laroche
Fly Away Home by Eve Bunting

96. A BOOK ABOUT BEARS
Bear and Wolf by Daniel Salmieri
The Valentine Bears by Eve Bunting
Winnie-the-Pooh by A.A. Milne
All Right Already! by Jory John
The Bear Who Wasn't There by LeUyen Pham
The Biggest Bear by Lynd Ward
Got to Get to Bear's by Brian Lies

97. A BOOK ABOUT YOUR BODY
Parts by Tedd Arnold
Usborne Look Inside Your Body
The Usborne Flip-Flap Body Book by Alastair Smith

98. A BOOK STARRING COMMUNITY HELPERS
Rescue Vehicles series by Valerie Bodden
Pull Ahead Books series
My Little Book of Rescue Vehicles by Claudia Martin
Big Mike's Police Car by Leslie McGuire
Lego City: Fight This Fire! by Michael Anthony Steele
Firefighters A to Z by Chris L. Demarest
Big Frank's Fire Truck by Leslie McGuire
Policeman Lou and Policewoman Sue by Lisa Desimini

99. A BOOK FEATURING A BIRD OR BIRDS

The 18 Penny Goose by Sally M. Walker
Mingo the Flamingo by Pete Oswald
Owl Moon by Jane Yolen
The Pigeon Finds a Hot Dog! by Mo Willems
Who Hatches the Egg? by Tish Rabe

100. A BOOK ABOUT A ZOO

If I Ran the Zoo by Dr. Seuss
Put Me in the Zoo by Robert Lopshire
A Day at a Zoo by Sarah Harrison

101. A BOOK ABOUT THE OCEAN

Cyrus the Unsinkable Sea Serpent by Bill Peet
Scuba Dog by Ann Marie Stephens
The Storm Whale by Benji Davies
Amos & Boris by William Steig
Davy's Dream by Paul Owen Lewis
Everything Goes: By Sea by Brian Biggs

102. A BOOK WITH JUNGLE ANIMALS

Safari, So Good! by Bonnie Worth
Usborne Beginners Animals books
The Ant and the Elephant by Bill Peet
Grumpy Monkey by Suzanne Lang
Jungle Doctor's Fables series by Paul White

103. A BOOK ABOUT SOMETHING THAT MAKES YOU HAPPY

What does your child treasure these days? If he's a budding coin collector, this is the perfect time to read a book on that. More of the run-around-outside type? How about a book on adventures? Hiking, tea parties, religion, babies, grandparents... nothing is off the table for this story!

104. A BOOK ABOUT YOUR STATE OR REGION

You choose—ask your local library, historical society, or homeschool group for ideas if you're stumped. This could also be a book about your geographical region: the prairie, the forest, the coast. Or, it could be about your city.

BOOK AWARDS & PARTY!

DO THIS AS SOON AS YOU FINISH YOUR READING CHALLENGE!

Grab your child's reading list from pages 28-33 and help him fill out the awards page (opposite page) to give his best and worst books an official award and mark them as most memorable this year.

Encourage him not to agonize over "was this one really the best..." but to go with his general impressions or write down all the contenders.

Send us a copy of this at books@timberdoodle.com and we'll be thrilled to credit you 50 Doodle Dollar Reward points (worth $2.50 off your next order) as our thank you for taking the time to share. We'll also congratulate your child on a job so well done!

Bonus Idea

Have an "awards ceremony" night all about one of the books on your list! You'll get the most specific ideas by searching online for "*book I picked* theme party," but here are some things to think through as you get started.

Food: How can you tie the menu to the theme? Green Eggs and Ham is easy—just replicate the food in the book! If you're working with a book that doesn't feature food directly there are a few options. Perhaps the book featured a construction crew. You could all eat from "lunchboxes" tonight or set up your kitchen to masquerade as a food truck. Or take the food you would normally eat and reshape it to match your story.

For instance, sandwiches can be cut into ships, round apple slices can be life preservers, crackers can be labeled "hard tack," and you're well on your way to a party featuring your favorite nautical tale.

Don't forget the setting, too. As ridiculous as it sounds, eating dinner by (battery-operated!) lantern light under your table draped with blankets will make that simple camping tale an experience your family will be recalling for years to come.

Or perhaps some handmade red table fans, softly playing traditional Chinese music, and a red tablecloth would provide the perfect backdrop for the story about a child's life in China.

The more senses you use, the more memorable you make this experience. Use background music, diffuse peppermint oil to make it smell like Christmas, dim the lights, eat at the top of the playground, or whatever would set this apart from a regular night and make it just a bit crazy and fun.

Don't get trapped in the "we must do this tonight" mode or in the "we can't do this because it won't be perfect" mode. Allowing your child to spend a few days creating decorations and menus is wonderful! Doing it today because it's the only free night on the horizon even though you can only integrate a few ideas into the preset menu? Also amazing! Your goal is to value the book and make some fun memories.

BOOK AWARDS OF

(YOUR CHILD'S NAME HERE ^)   (YEAR HERE ^)

I READ _____ BOOKS FROM THE READING CHALLENGE THIS YEAR!

FUNNIEST BOOK:

MOST MEMORABLE BOOK:

BOOK I READ THE MOST TIMES:

BOOK I LEAST ENJOYED:

TEACHER'S FAVORITE BOOK:

BOOK I MOST WISH WAS A SERIES:

CHOOSE YOUR OWN AWARD:

YOUR TOP 4 FAQ ABOUT NEXT YEAR

THINGS TO THINK THROUGH AS YOU ANTICIPATE SECOND GRADE

So, you're finishing up first grade already? How has it gone for you? Really, we'd love to know! (Plus, you get reward points for your review.) Just jump over to the First-Grade Curriculum page on our website and scroll down to submit a review.

As you look towards next year, there are a few things that you may want to know.

1. When Can We See the New Kits?

New kits usually release in April. Check our Facebook or give us a call for this year's projection, but it's always in the spring and usually April.

2. Free Customization

If your child has raced ahead in some subjects this year, or if you've realized you need to go back and fill in some gaps, or if you simply don't need more Math-U-See blocks, you'll be thrilled to know that you can customize your kit next year to accommodate that. You'll find full details on our website, but know that it is free and can often be completed online if you prefer to DIY.

3. Do I Need to Take the Summer Off?

Some students finish the grade with an eager passion to jump right into the next grade, and parents contact us asking if that's really okay or if they should take some time off so the child doesn't burn out. We are year-round homeschoolers, so we would definitely be fans of jumping into the next grade here!

However, the truth is that this is a decision only you can make. We can tell you that a long break can quench the thirst for knowledge, so if it were our child, we'd seriously consider moving right into the next grade. However, sometimes a little suspense makes the year begin with a beautiful anticipation!

If you decide to start early, you could consider saving one or two items for your official start date so that there is still some anticipation.

4. Can I Refill This Kit for My Next Child?
Absolutely! Each year's Additional Student Kit reflects the current year's kit (so the 2020–2021 First-Grade Elite Kit and the 2020–2021 Additional Student Kit correlate). If you loved it just the way it was, refill it now before we swap things around for next year. Or, if you prefer, wait for the new kits to launch and then let our team help you figure out what tweaks (if any) need to be made to the standard Additional Student Kit.

We're Here to Help!
If you have other questions for us, would like to share additional feedback, or would like to get in touch for some other reason, don't hesitate to drop us a line or give us a call. (FYI, we also have online chat on our website, in case that's easier for you.)

mail@Timberdoodle.com
800–478–0672
360–426–0672

DOODLE DOLLAR REWARD POINTS

WHAT THEY ARE, HOW THEY WORK, AND WHERE TO FIND THEM

If you're one of our Charter School BFFs, we just want to give you a heads up that the following information doesn't really apply to you. Doodle Dollars are earned on individual prepaid (credit cards or online payment plans are fine) orders and don't apply to purchase orders or school district orders. Sorry about that!

Now, with that out of the way, here's the good news. Almost any item you order directly from us earns you reward points! You will earn 1 point for every $1 you spend. 20 points = $1 off a future order!

Some families prefer to use this money as they go, while others save it up for Christmas or for those mid-year purchases that just weren't in the budget.

Can I Earn More Points?

Absolutely! Review your purchases on Timberdoodle.com to earn points. Add pictures for even more points!

We also usually have a few reward point events throughout the year, as well as our year-round Doodle Crew opportunities.

What Can I Spend My Points On?

Anything on our website. These reward points act as a gift certificate to be used on anything you like.

How Do I Get to My Points?

The simplest way is to look for the teal Doodle Dollars pop-up in the lower left corner of our website. Click it, login, then click All Rewards > Redeem and drag the slider to determine how many points to cash out. You'll immediately be issued a gift certificate to apply to your order. If you run into any challenges, please let our team know and we will be thrilled to assist you.

Check our website for the latest information on reward points:
www.Timberdoodle.com/doodledollars

CPSIA information can be obtained
at www.ICGtesting.com
Printed in the USA
JSHW021602260720
6862JS00006B/30